Lucid Living

IN THE
VIRTUAL AGE

JANE
BERNARD

Lucid Living in The Virtual Age

This book presents reasoning differently by utilizing intuitive skills to organically expand and transform self-awareness and communication. Our ability to maintain continuity with change, understand purpose and make a difference is constantly updated and balanced by what we sense. You can re-wire your thinking to use your whole brain by using cellular sensual tools when you eat.

Copyright © 2017 by Jane Bernard

All Rights Reserved.
Editor: RKedit
Title Logo Design: GIRVIN / Strategic Branding & Design
Design and Layout: R&J Pro
Production Supervison: Jane Bernard

Includes bibliographical references.

Library of Congress Control Number: 2017909024

Bernard, Jane

   Lucid Living in The Virtual Age.

   1. Philosophy. 2. Psychology. 3. Health. 4. Education.

ISBN-13: 978-0578192925
ISBN-10: 0578192926

Published in the United States of America by Transitions Press. LLC, Brooklyn, New York.

Inspiration for *Lucid Living* comes from Marshall McLuhan's philosophy about media and communication. Today, the way we reason and communicate is changing through our use of technology. Our thought evolution is a blend of wisdom and innovation.

The tech driven change in global communication is driving us to think with both sides of our brain. Texting with two thumbs at the speed of thought is an example. It's a subtle and powerful coordinated right/left side brain training that, like a gentle breeze, can become a tsunami.

The symbol chosen to represent sensual thinking throughout *Lucid Living* is a dorje, the Tibetan symbol of a lightning bolt. In my experience with Zen meditation, the epiphany on the cushion is referred to as "lightning enlightenment." Intuitive understanding for all of us is often this same sort of "aha" moment.

My desire is that *Lucid Living* brings flashes of fresh insight and self-awareness that will renew hope, nourish wonder and sustain enthusiasm for a better Life and healthier world.

I wish to thank Mary Kenner, my editor from RKedit, for her patient, reliable and thoughtful reading of my work. Bringing *Lucid Living* to completion was a team effort.

With respect,
Jane Bernard

Table of Contents

Introduction 7

Lucid Living 9

Chapter 1: Transformational Thinking 15

Chapter 2: Sensual Thinking 21

Chapter 3: Intuition, The 6th Sense .27

Chapter 4: Intuitive Tools 33

Chapter 5: An Appetite for Life .41

Chapter 6: Intuitive Eating 49

Chapter 7: Balance 57

Chapter 8: Duct Tape 61

Chapter 9: Stress 67

Chapter 10: Satisfaction 78

Chapter 11: Tough Love 85

Chapter 12: The Lucky Ones 92

Chapter 13: Sensual Syncing 106

Bio 109

Notes 111

Introduction

All the forces in the world are not so powerful
as an idea whose time has come.

Victor Hugo

Lucid Living is a simple handbook with the tools you need to think differently by using your senses. We cannot train our mind with our mind. The way to train our mind is through the passion and drive of what we sense. Sensuality is our skill of savoring, integrating and taking Life to a higher level. By eating intuitively, you can organically train your brain. Using your five senses with intuitive tools is the delicious and efficient way to transition from sensing to sensuality.

I am a philosopher and educator who naturally thinks outside the box. Working with children with learning issues taught me that the way to open and train our mind is through our instant ability to sense. What we sense creates inner synergy that our brain naturally responds to. Noticing what you sense organically focuses your brain and expands your mind.

Synergy is when energies come together and a new unified energy is born—like making a baby—or what happens when red and blue blend to make purple. The synergy between our senses and our mind creates action. What we see, hear, taste, touch or smell guides how we reason because we must sense something before our mind can recognize it. Intuition balances what we sense with what we feel and what we know.

For example,

> **NO SYNERGY:** You're crossing the street and a car's coming but you're distracted by something on your mind, your eyes are glazed, looking inward.

> **SYNERGY:** You're crossing the street and visually alert, your eyes signal your brain to flash danger and your heart immediately beats faster and your intuition steps in and balances what you sense (a car coming), with what you know from experience (dangerous) and what you feel (threatened) to create the action of stepping back.

By using natural sensuality to feel with your mind, you think with the whole brain. Ever felt curious? Curiosity invites new ways of problem solving. Ever made a connection with dignity? The feeling of dignity—as a decision guide—is often the source of unexpected revenue streams. Organic intuitive tools are our natural access to passion, creativity, wisdom and purpose.

My experience teaching people sensual thinking to lose weight, changed their lives unexpectedly. Self-image improved, relationships got easier and there was a new clarity about what mattered and how to achieve it. Insights into how emotional reactions interfere with real needs liberated people from years of habit. Life outlook opened. Weight management became an option. Sensual thinking is natural thought evolution.

Everything in our world is changing. Noticing what we see,

hear, taste, touch and smell keeps immediate options real and our thinking grounded. 21st Century thinking has special-effects and they are real. They don't fit into any categories we have experienced before, but we sense them automatically. Navigating in sync with change, and between virtual reality and lucid living we need to go to the ultimate limit of who we are by using sensual thinking. Experiencing an intuitive nudge or gut feeling focuses us in the direction of personal excellence.

Lucid living is being clear about who we are. Real life is the insane present that virtual reality is trying to perfect. Our senses keep us tuned to what's real. We may not be able to stay clear about what's happening tomorrow, but we can clearly be in-tune with personal values and priorities that bring excitement, security and peace of mind today.

While technology is leaping forward, humane conditions around the world are deteriorating. These are confusing times. Intolerance of all kinds is on the rise. Fortunately we have the answer. We can see, hear, taste, touch, smell and feel it. By using our whole brain we can stay clear about what's best to make smart choices. The future is ours to create. Sensual thinking is the powerful foundation of understanding and healing for our self, family and our world.

As you really taste dinner or experience lingering eye contact, Life changes. The deeper you sense, the more amazing it becomes. Intuitive understanding is a body/mind/soul connection that, like Love, is uniquely part our reality. Thinking sensually keeps us tuned to Life. That is our magic.

Lucid Living IN THE VIRTUAL AGE

This original way of thinking is for people ready to move forward with passion to create a future of their own design. Lucid Living is a highly-personal organic way to reason that drives ideas to actions. You are not limited by the past. By simply focusing with your senses, you can experience a direct and immediate difference in understanding how things come together. Importantly, you will automatically sense direction, timing and opportunity to take action that makes a difference. Goals in areas that matter most to you become clear and attainable. There is no emotional battle. This timeless and practical way of reasoning is organic. Children do it automatically. No formal education is required.

Your natural capacity to make a difference comes from within and is updated and balanced constantly by what you sense. Lucid living is a smooth way of understanding change that takes on new dimensions that provide unexpected power. Everything you sense updates your brain to propel you to take action and live richly. Easy to recognize intuitive tools are organic boundaries that keep you tuned to your values, and true to yourself. Sensual thinking takes Life to the next level. It's immersive, interactive, transparent reasoning that generates new conversations and entirely new possibilities in relationships, creativity and effectiveness.

Survival is our highest priority. In the organic search for understanding, resilience and drive, our mind, body and soul tune to energy of Love and sensuality. The second most sensual thing we do is eat. For this reason, the way we eat has high priority in our brain. Food is love—physically, emotionally and spiritually. To get what you need for personal achievement, stop pushing your mind. Instead, put the philosophy of Lucid Living into action and train your brain to tune to your vision and commitments, by eating intuitively.

The choice to be aware of what you sense is lucid power that is the beginning of action. The way we reason is part of the eco-system of evolution. You may want to do something and "know" you should, but be unable to motivate yourself to act. Without the balance of our senses, we are "afraid to leave our day job" or "need" to eat another piece of chocolate cake. We cannot push our mind to change. But, by eating intuitively, we train it to see things differently. Balance keeps us in the zone.

How we eat is how we communicate with the give and take of living. This book is not about dieting. It's about personal freedom that expands and transforms self-expression and communication. Effective communication is to the point, creative and affirms shared reality. By training your brain to think with intuitive tools when you eat, you take action that impacts broad-spectrum reasoning in profound and empowering ways. Life blossoms.

Don't be deceived by the simplicity of sensual thinking. Eating is a delicious way you energize and honor the essence of who you are. Because you eat every day, intuitive eating organically rewires your mind to rely on your values and priorities as portals to creating happiness.

The greatest answers and joys in Life are very simple. The future is yours to create. Sensual thinking liberates decision making from conditioning, dogma and emotional traps like stress. Lucid means being clear about what you stand for. It's peace of mind.

Chapter 1

Transformational Thinking

It takes a lot of courage to release the familiar and seemingly secure,
to embrace the new. But there is no real security
in what is no longer meaningful. There is more security in
the adventurous and exciting, for in movement
there is life, and in change there is power.[1]

Alan Cohen

Transformation means a dramatic change. It's transformational to think sensually because you are opening an unfamiliar approach to how you work, play and communicate. It's an unexplored immersive and interactive way of problem solving. Using all six senses brings multidimensional options and potential that you hadn't considered earlier.

This liberating transformation is you de-programming, re-routing and taking control of your thinking. As you notice what you sense, and use the intuitive tools, it's natural to feel inner balance and find understanding across the spectrum of change. With practice, you go from feeling restrained by dogma or stress to the comfort of understanding and trusting your own judgment.

Transforming the way you think by eating intuitively is brave.

It is like a caterpillar becoming a butterfly—with one major difference. A caterpillar eats for energy and Life and weaves her cocoon of change instinctively. There is no diet plan or challenging inner dialogue to inhibit the transformation. For us, transformation takes effort because we're accustomed to letting life's challenges and random inner dialogue dictate what we do. From childhood, we are culturally taught to reign-in our instincts.

Eating or thinking focused on a strict system or pattern causes an intuitive disconnect because it ignores messages from our body, mind and soul. It only takes a quick blink and a breath to notice what you sense and instantly tune to your body, mind and spirit. Really look at food when you think about eating. Notice the aroma. Have you tasted it before? Don't *think*. *Remember* with your senses. Healthy living is always a response to need.

Training your mind to be more productive, efficient and intelligent by eating intuitively makes sense. Eating and sex are the times we can be 100% in tune with our senses. Every great musician, artist, athlete and lover trains for quality organically through their senses. Artists, athletes and lovers practice, practice, practice. This is the way to be great. Eating intuitively is daily practice that reaffirms and realigns your sensuality with your mind. Are intuitive eaters better lovers? That's for you to answer. Sensual thinking is living life deliciously. It's the full experience.

All of us are born with unique powerful intuitive awareness of connections in our life and to our world. Lucid living opens the door to using the full power of our perceptual capabilities to interact with reasoning. Making brave choices takes reality to the ultimate limit of what we are capable of experiencing. It is our intuitive way of connecting with Destiny.

The moment you choose to be true to yourself—Life changes.

Bravery vitalizes and validates sensory connections to timing, pace and change. Sometimes change is raw; always, it's liberating. No one controls what you think, but you. This means you're responsible for who you are, where you're going, and why. The pace of Life is brisk. To be in the present, keep your eyes and ears open. Change never stops. No matter what's happening, your response and understanding has to maintain real connections with timing. Tuning to healthy change is leaving behind what no longer serves the big picture of your Life, to keep moving toward your future. You will find your rhythm.

> The only way to make sense out of change is to plunge into it, move with it and join the dance.
>
> *Alan Watts*

The path of opportunity and the sum of your potential are always available. Get your intuitive mojo working. Life is in front of you! Don't turn your vision over to someone else and don't waste it by thinking in a rut. So many people have hidden talents pushing against their skin. It doesn't feel pretty until we open up and live who we are meant to be. Taking the leap to think differently doesn't mean you are going to change the world, but it does mean you will leave a mark you are proud of.

"Thinking" without noticing what you sense is like being all dressed-up with no place to go. Sensual syncing keeps you on track, with gentle insights and protective boundaries; so you are heading in a healthy direction, to feel good, find the door, open a window, answer the call, meet the right person, or to just begin the journey.

Intuitive tools like courage, determination, curiosity or dignity open and refine communication. They are a very real brain-food that light-up Life in ways that guide and unite us all. It's very cool.

Emotional thinking is a response to conditioning or habits. Experience shows that emotions do not tend to guide the best decisions or always get desired results. The reason why is because habits and conditioning do not sync with change. Intuitive values you feel with your mind constantly sync with change, and guide decisions that fulfill self-identity and personal purpose. Noticing what you sense keeps thinking fresh.

Sensing is juicy, it's tasty. Thinking is dry, it's black and white. Living the full experience requires us to taste dreams, inhale desires and roll with our moments. If you feel jammed, then it may be a result of over-thinking. Imagine your brain is a sponge that is dried up by thinking and that it will expand with moisture of what you sense.

Develop multidimensional brain power by connecting with your sense of humor, your sense of joy and your sense of purpose. Talk less; sense more. No matter where you live or what you believe, sensual thinking delivers true presence. Respect, protect and excite yourself. Be intuitive.

Change drives need. The path to success is unpredictable. Insights created by the multi-dimensional focus of our senses, transcend time and experience to solve needs. Just like we are always breathing, everything in the world and in our lives, is always going through changes. Everybody gets unglued. Sensual thinking pulls us back together.

We need healing and satisfaction. Courage, curiosity, determination, dignity, honesty, humor and spontaneity are immersive intuitive tools that become answers—easy inner strength, good timing and innovation.

You demand a lot of yourself. You engage life physically, emotionally, socially, spiritually and intellectually. The conflict between real and ideal is constant. It's organic. Inner drive for change tunes to inner understanding and inspiration. Intuitively, you test boundaries to recognize and refresh your balance.

Sensual thinking is how we understand ourselves and connect organically with each other. You are already on your way. Change is always a fresh perspective. Be refreshed. Live out loud guided by your truth and be high on the gift of being alive. When we feel/think with our mind, we understand who we are. It's transformative to touch truth in our lives. It's how we 'get the message' to connect with each other and with Destiny.

Intuitive eating is deceptively simple. Focus on one meal at a time to get the most pleasure and nutrition from your food. Notice what you see, smell and taste. Check in with your body to see if you're really hungry. Eat just enough to feel good and trust hunger will return, and another meal will be found. When you focus on and appreciate what you eat while you eat, this is the physical foundation for healthiest digestion.

As you transform, use simple curiosity to notice how you feel and what matters. Depend on patience, determination and tenacity to protect yourself and you will be in tune with purpose. If change brings stress, dignity is the tool of trusting yourself that produces peace of mind.

According to Jay Dixit (Sr. Editor, *Psychology Today*), when changing eating habits:

> The hardest part is the first 72 hours when eating right is an act of will. After two or three weeks of sticking to it, your

hunger and cravings subside, and control over eating choices becomes automatic. ... Breaking out of your routine may make you more aware of your choices in general and less likely to engage in mindless eating[2] —

or mindless thinking.

Chapter 2

Sensual Thinking

We are travelers on a cosmic journey,
stardust, swirling and dancing in the eddies and whirlpools of infinity....
We have stopped for a moment to encounter each other,
to meet, to love, to share. This is a precious moment.
It is a little parenthesis in eternity.

Paulo Coelho

Our cosmic connections are unimaginable, but we enjoy them anyway. There are no limits to human potential but there are clear intuitive guidelines to be the best we can be. Sensual thinking delivers true presence that pushes Life up a notch. By thinking in sync with change instead of in-line with dogma, we tune to the bigger picture where there is a new version of the status quo. This doesn't change who we are, but it changes how we deal with change.

Sensual thinking is an immersive on-going energy boost of direction. Sensing is the stress-free zone of connecting. Tasting, seeing, hearing, touching and smelling are organic ways to truly grasp valuable connections and understand boundaries that bring purpose and satisfaction to choices. It's the difference between accepting blindly or choosing what makes sense. Sensual thinking with the intuitive tools that are explained throughout this book, is intuitive access to vibrant connections with understanding and peace of mind. It keeps decisions meaningful and Life exciting.

Despite plans, living happens spontaneously and Life gets tangled. No matter how busy you are, you live in your moments. Your senses drive every choice to keep your thinking on track. Purpose is an inside-out strategy. You know more than you realize.

Life is a time-stamped kaleidoscope of change. Nobody knows when their number is up. In the stream of change, opportunity can pass us by and we pay with low self-esteem. Being present with our six senses is a huge advantage.

We're taught to take our senses for granted. That is why until there's a crisis, we see, hear, taste touch and smell on auto-pilot. Sensual thinking is using the full experience of our mind to make connections.

It's so easy children do it automatically. They don't have to be liberated from dogma, old fears or conditioned doubts. But, we do. If you are not really 100% happy with the way things are working out, this is the opportunity to open your mind and sync with change. Rational thinking is not always satisfying because Life is not rational. Intuitively we search for insight and understanding that satisfies our Soul. It's good to feel satisfied.

Sensual thinking untangles obstacles by keeping us tuned to practical connections and the bigger picture. It zeros in on strategies that come from the heart There have always been inspiring leaders who were in-tune with Soul. Martin Luther King, Jr lived his dreams with passion, honor and dignity. Mahatma Gandhi noticed what he sensed, and used those insights to think with humility and determination to make global connections that established understanding. And, Steve Jobs used his senses to tap-in to the excitement of innovation. He got the whole world to "Think Different."

Natural soul is intuitive energy that helps us transcend the "irrational." It's how we fall in love with strangers and create solutions from debris. It's not religious or intellectual. Our senses bring the high-quality immersive ability to be objective. Our spirit brings us a sense of wonder, with the option to be great.

We sense change before we understand it. Everything we sense focuses our mind and touches our heart. What we see, hear, taste, touch and smell, grounds our thinking and frees us to be creative and passionate. Intuitive tools deliver true presence that exposes opportunities for increased productivity, enhanced communication and inner confidence to trust our self.

Noticing what you sense focuses your mind to relate to what matters in the moment. Sensual thinking is the organic way of rolling with change. Noticing what you sense is easy. Young children do it all the time. Sensual thinking reconnects with energy of the playful mind of your childhood. You will discover that you have an uncanny ability to focus objectively in any situation. Life becomes nearly stress-free.

Sensual thinking is the full experience of our minds. It is a strategy for successful relationships that begins with ourselves. The evolution of our thoughts keeps us tuned to personal character, purpose and love. Using intuitive tools to understand boundaries and sync with priorities delivers mental, emotional and spiritual stamina. It's a smooth, easy kind of balance. Imagine reasoning that "goes with the flow" because you understand what you need.

Thinking with your senses and feeling with your mind is high quality focus that enhances communication leading to increased productivity and satisfaction. Sensual thinking is boldness with a liberating back-up plan that is divergent and revolutionary. When you notice what you notice, answers are blowing in the wind. The only rule is: be honest with yourself about what you sense.

Besides seeing, smelling, tasting, touching and hearing the physical world, it's natural to sense what matters deeply for your happiness. There are lots of distractions. Intuitive boundaries clarify how things come together. They filter, focus and simplify an easy understanding of purpose.

Train your brain to think differently. Intuitive eating is the efficient, organic way to transition from sensing to sensuality. You will be savoring, digesting and taking Life to a higher level. Nothing is ever the way it has always been. With an open mind, you will feel forever young.

As you read this book, you are freeing your brain to think in sync with change. Consciously using intuitive tools to guide healthy eating decisions will program your mind to automatically apply these skills to all your thinking. You will discover renewed enthusiasm for fun. Change won't bother you. Sensual thinking is holistic understanding that feels like an easy confidence.

As one client put it, "Intuitive eating empowers you to be in control of how you feel. There is a mind-body sense of self-worth."

Intuition is the elephant in the room that people don't talk about. We have access to it and usually ignore it until we hit a wall or get a broken heart. In fact, no one regrets trusting their gut feeling. Sensual thinking is a stress buster that feels like common sense. Intuition is a nudge of Soul. Don't ignore the elephant. Stay connected to stability, safety, comfort, good health and Love.

It's exciting to be in sync with the big picture. Our minds and world are expanding. It feels good to let go of dogma from the past and step forward with sensual thinking. Go to the ultimate limit of what you are capable of experiencing. Like the great Dr. King, you can connect with your dream.

There is no doubt that by using sensual thinking, you'll discover how amazing you really are. Think different. Let common sense guide you through the small door of the improbable. The future starts now.

Life is 10% what happens and 90% how we react to it. Notice what you sense. Choice, not chance, determines the future.

Chapter 3

Intuition, The 6th Sense

Intuition will tell the thinking mind where to look next.

Jonas Salk

When it counts, people follow their intuition. Just ask any policeman, doctor, fireman or member of the armed forces. They trust intuition to know what's really happening. When it comes to intuition, everyone has it. Our six senses are the way we stay in touch with our body and our world. Intuition is the 6th sense.

Our five senses keep us in sync with the present. The 6th sense nudges us to be aware of priorities, purpose, direction and timing. Intuitively we tune to the bigger picture. When we stay tuned-in, we benefit.

Intuition links what we sense with what we know to balance actions with priorities. It's an organic protective head's up just like seeing, smelling, tasting touching and hearing. Since living is full of the unexpected and the impossible, it's smart take off the blinders. We need all our senses to navigate Life successfully.

Lucid living is visceral and direct. Intuition delivers true presence that serves us with dignity and curiosity to attain our highest potential. Instantly, we use it to sense timing, justice, purpose and place. We master our moments by thinking sensually.

Man your ships, and may the force be with you.[3]

George Lucas, Star Wars

Our "ships" are the five senses which bring us pleasure and protection by clarifying physical boundaries and connections. They ground and focus what we do and how we think by keeping us clearly in the present.

The "force" is our 6th sense. It's the surge of gentle energy we recognize as being in sync with inner values. Intuition grounds us with soul.

The 6th sense is a vital part of the puzzle of who you are. It balances what you know, with what you think and feel, to drive actions in sync with good health, good timing, purpose and Love. The more you respond to intuition, the stronger it gets. Like the other five senses, intuition is spontaneous and non-judgmental.

When you "man your ships," you're taking control of your senses by choosing to be completely aware of information you receive from them. This is especially easy to do when eating. As you tune-in to what you sense, you may notice what you take for granted, or you may feel more alert. When "the force" is with you, you know where you're going.

Intuitive eating connects meal-time pleasures with the satisfaction of being in sync with healthy Life-long priorities. It's relaxing because it's good for you. In the beginning, eating using your eyes, ears, nose, mouth and tongue is literally an eye opener.

Look at your hand and think of your five fingers as your five senses, and your palm as intuition.

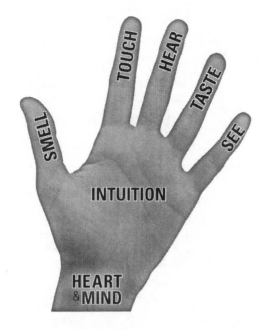

Your fingers work together because of your palm. The palm, like intuition, is a connector and an enabler. If you hurt your palm, it's hard to hold a glass. If you ignore your 6th sense, the other five senses cannot work together. This leaves you handicapped.

Intuition unifies and balances what you think and feel with what you sense, so that you respond fully to timing and needs. It is a focusing, arousing and grounding sense that infuses every experience with a vibrant big picture perspective that drives action.

What we sense is often easy to relate to, but hard to describe. Right now — you don't really know how your eyes are reading this, but you are. You don't fully understand how you hear music or the sound of a voice, but you do. We are always responding to energy and naturally accept what we sense. It's organic.

Observations are how we punctuate life. Every time you notice what you see, your perspective is refreshed—in an instant. At that moment, your brain relaxes and you see something new.

You never stop changing or evolving. But, if you fall out of touch with any of your senses, you are out of step with change and out of step with yourself. The 6th sense keeps us in rhythm.

Life is short. Use every meal to maintain your quality of Life. Intuitive eating is a lifestyle of finding pleasure in the benefits of eating, without the stress of dieting. Attitudes towards food and eating are mirrored in every relationship we have. If we are tense with the intimacy of eating, we're tense with other intimate acts. Instead of the pleasure of sharing together, we build personal resentments and self-doubts.

Intuition is not personality or intelligence. It's deeper and lighter. Our gut feeling is a soul connection that is part of every breath we take. Intuition is the quiet inner sense of direction that you recognize as being in sync with yourself. An intuitive nudge will reset understanding, passion and stability.

Our lives are a time-stamped gift of adventure. Intuitive balance is energy that feels like common sense. You may notice it as self-respect, courage, dignity, determination or love. Intuition guides us to understand the full experience of how things come together.

Everyone has experienced a nudge or gut feeling—it's the head's up to connect with the cosmos of our priorities. There are no limits to human potential but there are clear intuitive signals to be the best we can be.

Intuition is the elephant in the room. Experience the full capacity of your mind. Respond to what you sense. Taste what you eat. Sensual thinking will caress your soul until you peak. Don't be shy. Sense taste, timing, truth, justice and style and you will bond with belonging and see purpose. Smile with eye contact, and share a soul caress of insight. Your senses reset your brain to be insanely clear every time you use them.

How does eating intuitively train my mind?

Intuition is cellular connection that feels satisfying. It's not intellectual. By training yourself to eat intuitively, you are physically training the cellular memory of your brain to choose for satisfaction. Then, when you need a quick choice, intuitive thinking becomes a reflex.

Intuitive eaters see every meal as an opportunity to maintain their health. Health is wealth. Intuitive eating is protective, nurturing, social, and physically enjoyable. This positive focus snowballs into all communication and decision making. Your brain perceives intuition as logical, so there's no resistance. It makes sense to think with dignity when someone talks to you. It's intuitive to respond with curiosity to understand the whole picture. When things don't go smoothly, courage is a stress-free backup plan.

Listen to your *inner voice.*

Intuition is the inner voice. It's your organic, soul connection with purpose, self-control and confidence. The 6th sense is gentle and persistent. Sometimes it feels like common sense.

Trash *inner dialogue.*

We all experience emotionally driven, manipulative inner dialogue. Inner dialogue builds stress because it's usually destructive, restrictive or demeaning. It is what you have heard from outside yourself—the media, your mother, doctor, Life, etc.—repeated inside your head. Often inner dialogue doesn't feel intuitively "right."

There's an expression: Never judge a person until you've walked in their shoes. This also applies to you: Don't pre-judge yourself by what others think or say. Walk your own walk in your own shoes. Always choose your inner voice.

Factoid:

Dr. Alan Hirsch, neurologist, psychiatrist and Neurological Director of the Smell and Taste Treatment and Research Foundation in Chicago, has done studies on taste and weight loss which reveal the effect taste and smell have on the amount of food we eat. Dr. Hirsch discovered a trend where patients who had lost their sense of smell often gained 10 to 30 pounds.[4] As a result he theorized that if loss of smell leads to weight gain, the opposite might also be true—that enhancing smell can promote weight loss. And it does.

Chapter 4

Intuitive Tools

I have no special talent; I am only passionately curious.

Albert Einstein

Intuitive tools are the soul of lucid living. They are touch stones and signals that resonate from the deepest place of our understanding. Some people call it character, some call it soul. Love, justice, morality and wisdom are lights. Intuitive tools, that keep the lights shining, are easy to feel, natural to lean against and always the safety net.

The tools, listed below, are already a source of power within you. They guide with objective organization that disciplines your brain to achieve joy, self-respect and companionship. With them you can always sense the opportunity for unity, and the strength of inner conviction that leads to accomplishment.

As you will discover, it becomes automatic to depend on these healthy, fulfilling, invisible bonds that shelter, protect and empower Life. The way to cultivate your intuitive lifestyle assets, is by using them to maintain and improve understanding.

Start by depending on intuitive tools to make and keep choices in-line with your values. When uncertain about direction, use the tools to sync with perspective, control and purpose.

The tools refine thinking by using the immersive power of reality to make beneficial choices clear. They are a content filtering system that is relevant in any situation. Life challenges us to prove ourselves in surprising ways. Issues that connect with the values driving intuitive eating are deeply personal feelings of confidence, dignity, legitimacy and self-esteem. Yet, until we connect with sensual thinking, it's common to be barely aware of these powerful feelings.

Intuitive tools are timeless portals to the full power of our perceptual capabilities. Every leader and every survivor in every culture has depended on them for peak performance.

Our world is changing in ways we cannot imagine. Personal and social transformation go hand in hand. Intuitive tools are practical guides as we make the effort to use change to make life better.

You never change things by fighting the existing reality.
To change something, build a new model that
makes the existing model obsolete.

Richard Buckminster Fuller

Tool Summary

Curiosity is inborn boldness. It's an open mind that often begins creative thinking. It includes a flexible attitude about your body's needs. Being curious is how to stay in control of your options.

Prudence is like comparison shopping. It is balancing options to guide choices that serve your best interest. Prudence works with curiosity to clarify alternatives.

Tenacity is the inner drive of resolve—a commitment to be true to yourself, to be focused on your goals and honor your body, mind and soul. Tenacity is intuitive muscle power.

Dignity is an attitude of serene self-respect and self-mastery that is not found in what you do, but in how you do it. You feel it in your heart. Dignity maintains priorities.

Determination is energy experienced as an inner drive to follow through. Backed by tenacity, determination is "tough love" that powers through stressful situations to guide you forward.

Patience is a stress buster to count on for a clear perspective. It brings breathing room that helps end confusion. With practice, patience becomes a steady source of satisfaction.

Foresight is intuitive self-defense which stays connected with the present and the bigger picture at the same time. This way, you don't make choices you'll later regret.

Self-Discipline is transparent thinking that helps us be self-reliant and protective. It provides stability, self-esteem and momentum and is driven by dignity. Intuitive eaters use this tool to overcome disappointment.

Courage is part of the hidden spiritual agenda of living. It is an intuitive commitment to the truth. We don't need to justify it intellectually because we feel it. That's enough. Courage is your life-line. Tap into it anytime. It evaporates fear and overrides doubts. Courage is the sticking place.

The Mystery Tool (explained in Chapter 8) is invisible tape that holds together intuitive perspective and always shines on your to-tal potential.

Intuitive tools are visceral connections with personal character and style. Using them to fortify thinking, smoothly results in sat-isfying, rewarding momentum. With practice, they become auto-matic and you become an intuitive eater.

> Any sufficiently advanced technology is
> indistinguishable from magic.
>
> *Arthur C. Clarke*

To learn how people eat, I questioned people struggling with the ups and downs of losing weight and those who don't diet but are generally slim. The answers are surprising. I learned that eating is intensely personal.

One question I asked was: *When you look at a menu how do you choose what to order?*

Every dieter ordered for taste. This worked for me since I write about the senses, but my intuition kept nudging. Even though I related emotionally with the idea of going for taste, a bad feeling in my gut was making me edgy.

Finally, while talking to my girlfriend about a guy she was see-ing, I had an "aha" moment. She said that he had charisma, money and a sense of humor, but turned out to be a lying, cheating cad.

She looked me right in the eye and said, "You can't judge a book by the cover." Zing!

I finally "heard" my intuition. The taste of food is like the cover of a book. You can't judge a book by the cover and taste often misleads us about the *goodness* of food. As this thought steamrolled through my mind, I realized the relationship with food is like another personal relationship in my life—dating.

Before connecting with my intuition, I was emotionally driven in relationships. I've had amazing hot chemistry only to be dumped, and spent an evening being charmed, wined and dined only to find out the guy was married. In my search for the "one" I've learned to get past great chemistry, beautiful eyes and the flash of cash to reach the soul of who I'm seeing, or else pay the price of low self-esteem, frustration or a feeling of missed opportunity.

Entering a relationship with food, driven overwhelmingly by taste, is the same sort of a trap. If you know you aren't going to feel good afterwards, there must be something to prevent you from going there. Since seeing through the superficial lure of taste, smell and appearance is necessary to get to the soul of intuitive eating; I kept asking questions.

This is what I learned:

People who don't diet and are healthy share two surprising traits. First, they eat intuitively. They consciously use their senses and connect with their body at mealtime. Second, they use intuitive tools to guide eating choices in sync with their personal values.

They don't think about details of meals in advance. If they feel a need for carbs, they eat carbs. If they feel a need to lose weight, they cut back on portion size and modify eating to achieve short-term body issue goals. The tools make it natural.

Intuitive eaters eat to live instead of living to eat. They eat what they want and what they believe will bring them good health. They eat because they're hungry, not to fit a schedule. This sounds enviable to a dieter, but in fact, is easier than a diet because it's natural. Anybody can do it.

Instead of rules, intuitive eaters depend on tools to avoid stress, and stay clear about potential, opportunity, and change. The intuitive tools are convenient, useful, save time and money, and your body loves them. Does this sound like magic? Start using them and feel it.

Sensual thinking is multidimensional. The artist, Paul Gauguin, wrote, "I shut my eyes in order to see." If we only use our eyes when we eat, what are we tasting? Use all your senses with patience and determination to tune-in to what matters when you eat.

Intuitive tools are easy to sense and impossible to "think." You already use them to sense potent, phenomenal connections that drive you to experience understanding, purpose, belonging and joy. Thinking with intuitive tools while eating, organically trains your mind to use the tools to refine and clarify every situation.

Old thinking does not solve new problems. We thrive when we're in sync with what's happening now. Responding intuitively to change is our vital connection with self-control and purpose. For each of us, inner and outer world success depends on recognizing what is real and what is right. We don't need limits, we need direction. Intuitive tools are our reality check. They naturally filter out dogma, habits and fears from our thinking.

Having safe guidelines to make decisions you can trust is priceless. Intuition, like the truth, is independent. Sensual thinking is the skill of being in a crowd, without being part of the group mentality. It is thinking for yourself.

Intuitive tools keep personal priorities transparent. They are part of personal character. Character produces intangible energy we find in ourselves and that we admire and trust in others. It is the inner strength of invisible boundaries that attracts power, romance, personal satisfaction, and success. It is the part of our thinking where we balance sensuality with morality. You are a source of original energy and inside of you are the answers to your questions.

C – charm (is) *Irresistible*

H – health (is) *Rich*

A – awareness (means) *Tuned-in*

R – reason (perspective) *Smart*

A – action (means) *Being Decisive*

C – caution (protective) *Being Careful*

T – timing (when it's right) *Hot*

E – ease (doing what feels right) *Responsible*

R – rest (self-respect) *Loving*

We take our intuitive tools for granted until there's a crisis. Then, like a seat-belt, they are a lifesaver. Using them opens unexpected doors to the future. They are recognized, understood, and trusted ways of communicating and understanding across all boundaries by every culture in the world. Thinking sensually taps-in to mental, physical, emotional and spiritual stamina we all need to evolve.

Sensual thinking keeps us in touch with comfort zones, personal boundaries and unexpected opportunities. Intuitive tools train your brain by reconnecting you with natural skills you were born with.

> How different our lives are when we really know what
> is deeply important to us, and, keeping that picture in mind,
> we manage ourselves each day to be and to know
> what really matters most.
>
> *Stephen R. Covey*

Every person is born with the gem of intuition. Each intuitive tool is a facet of the gem. Polish your tools and let your intuition sparkle. Once you connect with the tools, rewarding choices become obvious and daily challenges stop being stressful. Intuitively there is nothing you can't do.

> Anything is possible if you've got enough nerve.[5]
>
> *J. K. Rowling*

Chapter 5

An Appetite for Life

Just as food is needed for the body, love is needed for the soul.[6]

Osho

Sensual thinking tunes-in to our appetites. We're born hungry for Love and understanding. To live we are dependent on an amazing body that is constantly processing and rebuilding. It is more efficient than a super computer. Hunger is a gift—it is our appetite for Life. Unwrap it with your senses and trust what you find.

Thinking sensually clarifies organic connections between appetites and needs. Intuitive eating is understanding yourself from the inside out. It is personal empathy. Understanding ways your body, mind and soul signal need, guides you to know yourself better. Things are often not what they seem to be. Intuitive tools train your brain to rise to the moment. You are never at a dead end. Because you don't know answers doesn't mean you cannot feel them.

Before you take another step, step back into yourself.
If you can govern yourself and be your own master,
yours is the whole wide world and
everything within it.[7]

Paul Fleming

Our thinking is always in flux, but priorities are stable. When you think you're hungry to eat, notice what you sense. Change is constant and your senses are tuned to the momentum. By noticing how your body feels, looking at food, and seeing and hearing your environment, non-food related issues and boundaries become clear. Eating intuitively is respecting your priorities.

Appetites are personal. It is intuitive to sense what takes Life to the next level. We recognize hunger through our state of mind. Thoughts reflect the pressures and realities of our day. Using foresight, prudence and curiosity, your head connects with your heart and body to tune your brain to good timing and healthy choices. In this way, you naturally satisfy your appetite for self-control and keep options open.

Using determination with your five senses, is an organic way to tune-in and understand your appetites. To eat intuitively you must look for what you *really* want. Appetites are not determined by a scale, clock or book. Instead, our bodies are always focused on healing and creating energy. This is what drives our food hunger. An intuitive pause to check-in with your tools brings breathing room to brake the cloying power of a stressful environment.

Using all six senses at mealtime clarifies physical needs and wholesome food boundaries. Intuitive tools expose purpose, clarity and direction that sync with your senses. Wake up your brain by noticing the fragrance of food before you put it in your mouth. Chew your food to *get* the taste and your digestive process is more efficient. Real nourishment is achieved when you're in sync with your whole self.

Experiment to see what satisfies your unique tastes and needs. Some people are hungriest in the morning. Others 'graze' eating small snack sized meals throughout the day. Still, every day is unique so notice what appetite you're feeding. Craving is often the same whether we are hungry for sex, food, understanding or excitement. Simple curiosity and dignity will modify eating choices and focus on intuitive drive for personal satisfaction. Fueling your body to produce comfort and energy is common sense.

Let food be thy medicine, and medicine be thy food.[8]

Hippocrates

How many times have we heard that food is Love? What does that mean? Are kisses fattening? Can a caress make you grow? What is this love that nurtures three times a day? Healthy eating will give us energy to feel joy, fulfill our responsibilities and notice that Life is a gift. It is always a response to a physical need.

Sometimes love is eye contact with that special person while you're eating, or sharing ice cream and talking about the way it feels in your mouth. Our social appetite for Life is magical. We hunger for power, connection, respect and understanding.

Appetites are signals. Love yourself.

Trust your senses and trust yourself. Intuition is never self-destructive. But, it's not predictable. Like Adele, you may need to *set fire to the rain* or, you may be hungry for conversation, entertainment or sleep.

Be curious and use tenacity to know what pushes your buttons around food. It's easy to misjudge the amount we eat. Experiment to understand what satisfies your unique physical hunger cycles and body rhythms.

If you don't know when you're hungry,
you don't know when you're full,
so you won't know when
to stop eating.[9]

Elisabetta Politi, RD

When it comes to physical hunger, things are always changing. There is no need to memorize answers. Be curious. Sense what feels right, to get out of your head. Stress is a mental boxed-in feeling. Exit stress with an intuitive pause to check in with the full experience of your mind.

- What is my state of mind? Thinking is overrated, so notice what you sense.

- Why do I feel hungry? Learn the signs. The fact is you may need a hug, not a hamburger.

- What is my appetite telling me? Notice what you're seeing, hearing, tasting, touching, feeling and longing for. The present is awesome.

- Don't be bullied by social pressure to eat. Instead, let self-discipline, integrity and natural dignity guide your behavior.

- Be gracious and respectful of others.

- Enjoy what you eat.

- Don't feel obligated to "clean your plate."

- Eat small but nutritionally satisfying portions. If you're comfortable with yourself, everyone else will be, too.

- If someone makes a negative comment about your choices, smile and say you are following your intuition. No one can argue with that.

Intuitive eaters watch everything they eat. Before beginning to eat, they observe what kind of hunger their body feels and what's on the table. Good choices kick in "automatically."

Use curiosity and foresight to identify emotional distractions that feel like hunger. There is an expression: "To be forewarned is to be forearmed." Foresight reveals the impact of stress on your eating and gives the advantage of a long-term perspective.

Intuition is never negative or hostile. An intuitive nudge always focuses on your long-term priorities. When negative inner dialog creates doubt, use sensual thinking bring back control.

> Whether you think that you can, or that you can't,
> you are usually right.[10]
>
> *Henry Ford*

It's easy to confuse hunger with stress or depression. Stress triggers the hunger hormone, ghrelin. Ghrelin is related to our survival instinct.

> Until modern times, the one common human experience was securing enough food to prevent starvation. Our hunter-gatherer ancestors needed to be as calm and collected as possible when it was time to venture out in search of food, or risk becoming dinner themselves. . . . The anti-anxiety effects of hunger-induced ghrelin may have provided a survival advantage.[11]
>
> *Dr. Jeffrey Zigman, researcher at UT Southwestern.*

> Pay attention to your body. The point is
> that everybody is different.
> You have to figure out what works for you.[12]
>
> *Andrew Weil, MD*

Factoids:

- Physical hunger will nudge relentlessly when your body needs any element of nutrition. It could be as obvious as protein or as obscure as a trace mineral deficiency.

- If you're still hungry after a meal, it doesn't mean you need more of the same food. For example, you eat a hamburger and fries for dinner and are still hungry. Having another hamburger, even without the bun, is not the answer. It may be something as simple as eating a pickle or you may be thirsty. Be prudent and bold; consider your options.

- When physically hungry, the feeling doesn't go away if you wait it out. If emotionally hungry, often doing something distracting satisfies your real need and the craving disappears.

- It's best not to eat food closer than two hours before you go to sleep because your stomach needs time to digest it. The digestive system works for hours after you stop putting food in your month.

- Digestion and sleep are not designed to occur at the same time. The best night's sleep occurs after the work of digestion is completed.

- Food is fuel and sleep is the battery that recharges your body for continued use. You can have a full tank but feel tired if you need to recharge. Instead of overeating, try a power nap for 10 to 30 minutes for the boost that sparks.

- I like pickles and looked up the nutrition facts for eating one pickle on: http://www.nutritiondata.com/. This useful website for practicing the tool of curiosity, states that one pickle spear is a good source of vitamin A, potassium, manganese, dietary fiber, vitamin K and calcium. I discovered that pickles are anti-inflammatory — I also learned they can be high in sodium.

Chapter 6

Intuitive Eating

The way we eat mirrors the way we think. Intuitive eating is highly tuned to Life. It's reasoning with dignity and character to achieve your highest potential. Eat for good health and you find satisfaction and energy. Consider eating to be an investment in the future and consider your options. Choose for success.

Intuition is an immersive interactive asset that channels the full power of your potential. Sometimes it feels like passion. Intuitive understanding is cellular, not intellectual. Like fitness, intuitive eating has body/mind connections. It is an encompassing lifestyle tuned to the variety of your needs and natural physical changes. Using intuitive tools creates enduring motivation by providing a value driven environment. The rewards of intuitive eating are both psychological and physical.

Intuition is not a way of thinking. It's an organic way of being tuned-in to change that makes smart choices a priority. Ignoring it keeps you out of touch with signals from your body and your heart. When you eat intuitively with your five senses and the tools, choices may not be what you expect, but they will work.

Because developing physical potential from the inside out is intuitive, intuitive eating is an efficient strategy for training both body and mind. Long-term benefits include a healthier body, more productive lifestyle and a clearly present mind.

Eating intuitively is personalized support, strategy, and action plan for long-term fitness. The first step is to decide that you want to recognize your intuition. It's that simple; intuition is as easy to recognize as it is to ignore.

Eating impacts everything—our sex drive, the health of our skin, how clearly we think, etc. Eating intuitively sustains personal satisfaction, physical comfort, and the energy to deal with stress. Sensual thinking is easy flexibility, focus and a relaxing attitude in how you approach choices and responsibilities.

Anyone can use intuitive tools to decide what works best for them. If you're a dieter, intuitive eating puts an end to the relentless cycle of over-eating, guilt and deprivation. But, losing weight is not the focus here. Instead, it is a healthy, balanced, intuitive relationship with food and eating.

Notice what you see, hear, taste, touch and smell for five minutes, and your whole day will change. Your senses reset your mind. Intuitive eating with the ten tools trains your brain to be insanely clear.

Eating connects with all appetites: a hunger for comfort, a craving for love, a passion to understand who you are, and a thirst to know how to protect yourself and live the best quality of Life. All of this is visceral and direct. Life happens in the present.

If you pay attention to how food smells and tastes you will eat 22% less.

Dr. Alan Hirsch

Q & A:

What is intuition?

Intuition is the inner drive that maintains values and priorities. It connects and balances needs of heart, mind, body and soul. Count on it as a clearinghouse to keep you on track with eating and Life challenges.

What is intuitive eating?

Intuitive eating is coordinating what you sense with what you know to satisfy healthy eating goals. It's custom-tailored reasoning filtered by your five senses and refined by the intuitive tools. The benefit of intuitive eating is a long-term reality, including maintaining long-term weight control.

Can I use my Intuition to lose weight?

Absolutely yes—unless you are already thin.

What about diets?

Dieting and deprivation just don't work. Sometimes the diet works, you lose weight and it stays off for a while. But reality is that 98% of those who do lose weight put every pound back on, with a staggering 9 out of 10 weighing more 5 years later than they did to begin with! If you are fed up with dieting or controlling what you eat, if you want to find a way to eat when you're hungry and get on with your Life—intuitive eating is definitely for you.

Does everyone have intuition?

Yes, everyone is born intuitive. When you feel in sync with yourself, you are in touch with your intuition.

Why do some people seem to have better intuition than others?

Some people trust their intuition more than others. For example, police, soldiers, nurses and artists all tend to rely on their intuition.

How can eating be intuitive?

Eating is part of your survival instinct. Nothing is more basic or more intuitive than the will to live. Every animal has it.

Does every animal have intuition?

No. Only people have intuition. However, every animal is born with strong instincts. Instinct is spontaneous and doesn't involve thinking. All animals except us live by their instincts- and we're the only ones that diet.

What is the difference between instinct and intuition?

Instinct is a kind of clarity and intuition is a kind of focus. Instinct is a part of nature, so when you trust your nature, you will tune into your instincts. Intuition is a coordinating and guidance system inside of you that connects with reasoning.

What about a "gut feeling"?

A gut feeling is usually an intuitive response. If you have a gut feeling you can use the tools to know whether intuition is protectively guiding you, or if it is guilt or another emotion pushing your button.

How do I know if it's my intuition?

Intuition is never destructive. It will never guide you to do something destructive to your body. Just like your 5 senses: sight, smell, taste, touch, and hearing, your intuition will protect you or lead you to a pleasurable experience. If you think your 'gut feeling' is to eat a 2nd or 3rd huge slice of pie, or an entire box of cookies, or a whole quart of ice cream, think again. Something else is pushing you to do things that hurt your body and ultimately your self-image. Once you master the tools for staying connected with intuition, you will be able to screen out manipulative emotions. You will be in control at mealtime.

How can intuitive eating make me aware of portion control or healthy eating?

Because intuition is the clearing-house for experience as well as what you feel and sense, portion control and eating what your body needs becomes natural.

What is the best way to fine tune my senses?

Just notice what you sense. You can do it at any time. Look into the eyes of someone you love. Drink a cup of hot tea. Eat a ripe peach, or walk through the supermarket. It can be a new experience.

Dieters see each meal as a step along the path to a long-term weight loss goal. Intuitive eaters see each meal as an immediate important source of energy and nourishment. The intuitive goal is a lifestyle of maintaining a comfortable, healthy body.

Planning dieter meals a week in advance is counter-intuitive. It's impossible to know on Monday what your body will want or need for lunch on Wednesday. Sensual thinking tunes to the present, which is where your body is all the time.

The word "diet" originated in the 14th century to describe the restricted intake of prisoners. "They were fed a diet of bread and water." This is the 21st century. Today, every species except ours eats intuitively. Note: We're the only ones who diet and we're unhealthy because of our eating habits.

According to an article in the *New York Times*, if we force our self to eat something boring or unappetizing, our body absorbs up to 70% *less* nutrition.[13] It's healthiest to enjoy what you eat.

Thinking about eating strictly in terms of calories and rigid diets keeps you focused in your head and misses the point of connecting with your body. It's not intuitive.

Everyone, at least once, suddenly has intuitively jumped out of harm's way. A study done by the Army Research Institute confirms that in a dangerous situation, intuition sends out an alarm so you react physically before understanding in your mind and recognizing why. (Dr. Jennifer Murphy, IED Study, Army Research Institute, 2009)

The fact is nobody rules your thinking or your body but you. Every meal you eat is personal and custom-tailored by you for your needs. Intuitive eating frees you to make choices that feel right. Sensual thinking keeps your reasoning fresh.

If you can't solve a problem,
it's because you're playing by the rules.[14]

P. Arden

Exercises to be an intuitive eater:

- Use your senses. Notice how food you're eating looks, smells and tastes. Notice if your body is relaxed or stressed. Only eat to satisfy hunger.

- Smell food before putting it in your mouth. Does it smell inviting? Greasy? Fresh? Bad? Be curious. Learn about what you're eating by smelling it. If the food doesn't smell right, it isn't. Let your nose protect you and help guide choices.

- Taste food as you chew it. The digestive process starts in your mouth. Chewing burns calories. We taste more when chewing with our mouth closed. It's sensual thinking to taste food and enjoy it.

- Be thankful for your meal. Think about what food is giving you: energy, strength, health, nourishment and pleasure. Your body will relax and you will get more nourishment from your food.

- It takes 15 minutes before your brain gets the message from your stomach that you've eaten. Be patient. Take time to have conversations when you eat and you will eat less. Talk about the food. Share the pleasure of taste.

- Visualize and feed your ideal healthy body when you eat.

Use your senses to develop your taste in a way that makes sense for your lifestyle and eating goals. If you want to eat less, try:

- Instead of eating candy, have a sliced apple; it probably

costs less than the candy bar and will fill you up longer.

- Instead of French fries, eat a baked potato.

- If you crave carbs but want to lose weight and have plateaued, break the dinner roll in half, then break it in half again and slowly eat a quarter of it instead of the whole thing. Have the remainder of it removed from the table.

- It's common to mistake thirst for hunger. Instead of eating in the middle of the night, drink half a glass of water—even if you don't think you're thirsty. Water is healthy. It's good for your skin. Your body uses it to flush out impurities and there are no calories.

- Juice has as many calories as soda, so limit intake to 8 ounces per day. Try diluting juice with water; it will last longer and you will benefit from drinking more water and less sugar.

- If you tend to eat fast and to eat big portions, try to drink a full glass of water before each meal. This will slow you down.

Our relationship with food is highly personal. Emotionally you may justify eating a piece of cake at midnight because you "deserve it." What you deserve is to feel loved. Putting food in your body that will distort your appearance, disrupt your sleep or make your stomach hurt is not an act of love, it's perverted hostility. Notice what you sense to connect with a clear picture. Be kind to yourself.

Do you still feel it is hard to make healthy eating choices? It becomes hard if there is a disconnect from our senses. Many habits that are socially and commercially ingrained, ignore our heart, mind and body. Using your senses and intuitive tools opens your mind to shed confusing habits that do not serve you.

Chapter 7

Balance

It's the possibility of having a dream come true
that makes life interesting.

Paulo Coehlo

Staying balanced in the stream of living is a skill. When we're "off," there is an edgy feeling, a nudge or even a sense that "something" is missing. Emotions can work for or against us. By balancing emotion with reason, chances to be fulfilled are dramatically improved.

Sensual thinking is the natural power base that takes Life to the next level. It's very simple. We have six senses that drive balanced action to keep Life in focus. This is multitasking we are born to do.

Our intuitive foundation for long-term happiness is a combination of focus and flexibility. By using our senses to focus on the moment, the effect is like a magnifying glass revealing connections that make things stand out we might otherwise gloss over. To maintain balance, thinking sensually guides our brain to adjust to constantly changing immediate needs, while staying focused on long-term priorities.

When driven by emotional reasoning, the mind is a trickster—

rationalizing and justifying choices. When thinking narrows to an emotional point, we fall out of touch with our senses and lose perspective. This has nothing to do with a lack of intelligence, but the negative impact is the same. It happens to all of us.

An easy breathing technique creates a "safe place" where we can feel clear-headed and inwardly strong. Because our mind responds to words, choose a simple word as a trigger. I like the word, "pause." Quietly saying "pause" and simultaneously taking a few deep breaths in and out, will immediately re-balance your thinking. Practice this technique to refresh focus and re-establish natural mind, body, soul momentum at any time. Fresh focus is the freedom to make a fresh choice.

Time brings responsibilities and demands. People depend on us. We have to respond to a swirl of duty, deadlines and decisions. The fact is, everything you do makes a difference. Commit to sensing more in the moment and your thinking becomes sharper and clearer. This makes it easier to balance strong emotions that often come with stress. Plan for success. Use sensual thinking in this natural way to honor, enjoy and empower your body and mind.

Every meal and every plan can be modified based on what is happening in your Life. When you eat, the idea is to nourish yourself, get energy and maintain your healthy image. Emotional bullies like denial, anger, bargaining and depression throw us off-balance. These are brought under control by thinking sensually. Using the intuitive tools to focus on what makes sense, directly balances perspective freeing your mind to respond to priorities.

Using flexibility and focus to eat wisely:

- Eat only if you're hungry. There's no other reason to eat.

- Eat only what you want. Hint: You want what you need.

- Our body is clearly a source of pleasure. Feed your body what feels good.

- Never take hunger or your body for granted. Approach each meal as if it's the only one.

- When uncertain, pause with a breath to relax and re-focus.

- To avoid overeating, eat slower. Try to notice when you've had enough. Then stop putting food in your mouth. Allow your body and brain time to work together.

- Don't multi-task. When eating just eat, don't drive, walk, work or watch TV. Ignoring your body leads to overeating.

- Notice how you feel about yourself. When you feel in sync, you're using your intuition. It's as simple as that.

Don't judge yourself. It's human to make mistakes. Recognize them, learn from them and let them go, and you will feel balance.

As you practice intuitive eating you'll sense increased self-control. It's exciting. When you get excited, you're on a roll and when you're on a roll, it snowballs. Eating intuitively becomes a rhythm of balance and satisfaction.

- Success comes by acting on what we understand. Progress and change are naturally slow because growth is organic. You are evolving. The good news is that it may well be permanent.

- Ultimately, to get the full experience of your mind, maintain a determined commitment to follow through. Think with your senses and depend on the intuitive tools for direction. Answers you seek are inside of you. You know much more than you realize.

- Dreams can come true.

Being in tune with what's meaningful and taking action that makes sense is the path to personal excellence. The more we use our senses, the higher our levels of sensitivity. It becomes natural to do the right thing, the right way, with no regrets.

Seek the truth and don't sweat surprises. Personal integrity is the bedrock of happiness. Simple physical sensitivity builds moral courage that takes us beyond who we have been.

In the college of Life, no one escapes the laws of balance. Being balanced is staying in the zone. It's lucid living.

Chapter 8

Duct Tape

Grace and gratitude are the duct tape of intuitive tools. They will fix anything. Grace accepts weakness and strength without judging. Gratitude finds enthusiasm and momentum that drives us to achieve goals. Together these bring a lucid perspective that stabilizes understanding and personal success.

By holding us together beyond our comfort zones, grace and gratitude reinforce flexible intuitive reasoning that drives both creative thinking and natural momentum. Whether we need a lucky break or to plan a party, grace and gratitude work with our five senses to guide us to recognize inspiration.

Grace is when caring connects with courage. We use it intuitively when we cross our fingers for good measure. Sometimes it feels like faith. It is always present to reinforce our foundation. Success is the result of persistent action. If you don't see what you need the first time, use tenacity and look again. You will uncover solutions you need. Gratitude will hold them together.

Grace and gratitude work together like our hands. Grace is the tool that creates understanding that leads to happiness. It is personal forgiveness that keeps us receptive to change. While grace leads to happiness, gratitude is the tool that connects us with continuity, which is the source of balance that makes us feel complete. The sense of completion is soothing and personal. It brings sureness to thinking that guides us to sync with enthusiasm, good timing and each other.

What we put in our body or in our mind can empower or disrupt all aspects of Life. Eating habits mirror the ways we make choices. Whether you are deciding what to eat for dinner or who to spend the evening with, an attitude of gratitude leads to intuitive insights by refreshing the inner rhythms of self-control.

> Continuously stretching ourselves will even
> help us lose weight, according to one study.
> Researchers who asked folks to do something different
> every day—listen to a new radio station,
> for instance—found that they lost and kept off weight.
> No one is sure why, but scientists speculate that getting
> out of routines makes us more aware in general.[15]
>
> *M. J. Ryan*

Simple sensual awareness delivers the full experience of our minds that builds personal power. By focusing on what we sense in the present, pathways in our brain are refreshed to provide spontaneous, healthy reasoning. Be grateful that you have clean air to breathe. Notice how beautiful love is. Be thankful that you can think for yourself.

> Knowing what you're good at and
> doing more of it creates excellence.[16]
>
> *M. J. Ryan*

Duct tape can fix anything. Grace and gratitude bring flexibility, consistency and momentum to reasoning that ease and encourage every chance to succeed. Like light, Grace shines on potential and forgiveness, and like your sense of touch, it is always present.

Life is what we make it, always has been, always will be.

Grandma Moses

Lucid living is a contract to be at your highest potential in every situation. Grace constantly recharges this natural experience. Set no limits on your dreams.

Be patient with everyone, but above all with thyself.
Do not be disheartened by your imperfections,
but always rise up with fresh courage.[17]

St. Francis de Sales

Don't be afraid of what you cannot do. Fear is one of those unconscious habits that are ruts. Depend on grace and gratitude to hold foresight and determination together and to transform fear into focus. You will find what you need. Every step forward focused on the next correct action, keeps the future open. Be gentle with yourself. Life is big. Grace supports your ability to see the big picture, no matter what it is.

Never be in a hurry. Do everything quietly and in a calm spirit.
Do not lose your inner peace for anything whatsoever—even if your whole
world seems upset.[18]

St. Francis de Sales

Because they could not imagine giant white birds coming across the waters, it is said that the American Indians could not see Columbus's ships approaching the mainland until they landed. The concept of sailing ships and another continent were out of their range of experience.

Visualize your dream life and your dream body. Like Columbus's ships—it may be right in front of you. Trust that you will achieve your intuitive goals. Inner grace will point to opportunity and the amazing.

When knowing the truth is not easy, grace seeks it out. The truth holds Life together. The process of responding to the truth is continuous. As you move forward and achieve your goals, you'll discover that facing the truth is like breathing—you can't stop. You will be smiling with gratitude.

> How do you measure a year in a life?...
> In daylights, in sunsets, in cups of coffee.
> In inches, in miles, in laughter, in strife...
> Measure in love.[19]
>
> *Rent, Jonathan Larson*

Responsibilities, challenges and opportunities change all the time. An attitude of gratitude keeps us stable. Through it all, the organic drive of courage, foresight, curiosity and prudence connects with the inner appetites of our mind. We are naturally hungry for purpose, stability, safety, comfort, good health and Love. These are the appetizers, main course and desserts of living.

It's easy to use grace and gratitude to understand change and tap into natural enthusiasm. Grace is part of your natural charisma. Give yourself every chance.

Knowing yourself is to discover a sparkling gem. It's worth the effort.

Chapter 9

Stress

Stress jams our ability to reason. It makes us vulnerable to being seduced by food. You might eat to avoid thinking about what's stressing you, or obsess over food and gorge without mercy. When stressed we miss the exit, forget appointments, lose our keys and make decisions that are not smart. However, sensual thinking is mnemonic. Mnemonic (ni-MON-ik) means, "assists the memory." Noticing what you sense improves your short and long term memory.

Sensuality and stress are not compatible. That's why music is relaxing and beauty makes us smile. Sensing is organic *feng shui* that relieves stress, unclutters mind-space, and allows time for living.

Time is the essence of Life. It's all we have. No one knows when their number is up. With limited time to follow our bliss, pay bills, achieve our dreams and enjoy each other, it's smart to think sensually. Everyone has a timeline, needs and stress. Sometimes stress signals a craving for the irrational just because we need a break.

The fact that logic cannot satisfy us awakens an almost
insatiable hunger for the irrational.

A. N. Wilson

Our senses diffuse stress with wonder. Sensuality grounds us with perspective along the way that frees natural creativity. The sensual experience of wonder does the impossible. It connects us with what is bigger than ourselves by tuning in to natural reality.

Wonder does not connect with dogma, rules or logic, but it strongly connects us with freedom, music, change and each other. Even when stressed, it's easy to notice what you sense. Why not enjoy a liberating connection with the irrational? Let the wind whisper in your ears. Lick your spoon the next time something is delicious. The more you think with your senses, the more lucid your connections and the more amazing your mental focus. Wonder is an explosion of connection. It's the sperm connecting with the egg. We don't need to understand it. It's real.

Stress drives us to lose perspective. Stay true to yourself. No matter what is happening, you must move on. Everything you do matters. Depend on courage and patience to focus your energy. Life is rarely predictable but stress is avoidable. Be curious. There are no limits to how things can come together.

Our senses stream with winds that blow straight through time. Natural sensuality is a symphony of rhythms that takes us beyond ourselves. Stress, however, is a stagnant experience.

Sensual thinking frees our mind to turn stress from a liability to an asset. It gives us tools, not answers, so we can think for ourselves. It's our choice to change, grow, accept what's happening or stop it.

Simple curiosity is gentle creative thinking that is part of every solution. Look for it. Don't let stress inhibit clear thinking. If you sense an energy drain that narrows or diverts reasoning from productive, bigger-picture thinking, or if you experience inner imbalance—it's stress. Breathe and check in with your body. An intuitive nudge turns the key to unlock a stressed mind and body.

Wonder is the beginning of wisdom.

Socrates

Be determined to override stress by thinking sensually and the big picture will come into focus, bigger than you remember. The world will unfold with new rhythms. Problems will get smaller. Time expands when you are aware of what you sense. Then, happiness happens. Natural reality is not complicated.

Responsibilities create stress. When that stress makes us sharper, it's an asset. We don't have to be heroes but we do have to responsible for our choices. Challenges help us rise to the occasion. Eating intuitively directly connects our mind and body with life-giving priorities. This puts inner-voice stress on-hold.

Stress is often caused by thinking in terms of limits. For example, "I don't have enough time, money, connections, sleep, food, clothes, etc." This type of thinking signals it's time for an intuitive pause. When we're clear about where life's questions and challenges come from, it's easier to solve them.

Sometimes stress comes from the system. I believe 90% of rules are designed to expire. They should come with a time-stamp. Generally, rules are created to solve a problem or correct confusion. Good rules fix the problem.

For example, with dieting, you may decide to have desserts only on weekends as an experiment to gently lose weight. You make it a rule. It becomes a handrail to keep you on track and then it becomes an automatic part of you. You feel a calm, healthy sense of accomplishment. The rule has done its job.

Rules made for breaking are the ones that serve no purpose. They are ones that feel tedious or stressful. We need to let go of them to see what needs fixing and what doesn't. Today, nearly everywhere, rules are "broken" because they no longer make sense. It's time to think outside the box. Problems like everything else, change. It is part of the topography of living.

Stress is part of the cultural agenda. Protect yourself. Your sensuality is stronger than stress. Use lucid living to see solutions. Allow yourself to tune-in to what you smell, listen to the words you hear, notice how you feel, and what your eyes are hungry for.

Reality is spontaneous and always changing. Values like dignity and curiosity are constant. When you know you've done the right thing for the right reason, satisfaction cannot be taken from you.

Intuitive eating keeps reasoning smooth despite stress. Allowing your mind to naturally respond to what you see, hear, taste, touch or smell, reasserts priorities in your brain. Use sensual thinking to go from being stressed to being insanely clear.

Let breathing help relax your body. Inhaling deeply, at least twice slowly, is organic action that rapidly releases stress. This is especially important when we eat. If our body is tense, the digestive process can be thrown off.

Prolonged stress created by rigid thinking, brings imbalance to our immune system, encourages hypertension, heart disease, sleep disorders, and more. Did I mention overeating? Diets are, by definition, restrictive. Feeling restricted fuels stress.

Stride toward relaxation by talking less and sensing more. The moment you recognize what deeply feels right, that inner confidence strengthens and propels you forward to where you belong.

A curious mind often finds new options. If you feel unsure of what you need, shred the stress. Do a workout with the intuitive tools and your five senses. This exercise will help you think smarter, see beauty, taste food, smell change, and detect lies. The more you use the tools, the stronger your insights become. Sensual thinking is a reality check that keeps the flow clear. It constantly, organically expands your mind.

Consider laughing a stress buster. A good laugh, like eating an apple a day, keeps the doctor away. Studies have found laughter activates our most protective immune cells, increases blood and oxygen flow through the body and manipulates hormones! It's an organic vitamin.

> Studies show that the physical act of smiling
> can signal your brain to halt the negative,
> mood-altering effects of stress.
>
> *Roz Trieber,*
> *educator, author, HumorFusion.com*

Sensuality is fun that spontaneously invigorates us. Smile at yourself, take an intuitive pause to recognize and regain your relaxed, balanced perspective. Enjoy the moments.

Chronic stress activates the hormone, ghrelin,[20] which incorrectly tells the brain that we're hungry. Dr. Jeffrey Zigman, University of Texas Southwestern Medical Center, notes: "An unfortunate side-effect (of ghrelin) is increased food intake and body weight."

"Our findings support the idea that these hunger hormones

don't do just one thing," his associate, Michael Lutter, adds. "Rather, they co-ordinate an entire behavioral response to stress and probably affect mood, stress and energy levels."

When we stay clear about the big picture, mind, body and soul equally support each other to guide lucid living. To escape unhealthy stress:

- Be honest with yourself about what you feel.
- Connect with what you sense.
- Use the intuitive tools to clear your thinking.

When conversations become stressful, a dignified attitude with a light smile is usually a stress buster that re-establishes boundaries and relaxes emotional knots. But if social tension mounts, excuse yourself to go to the restroom for an intuitive pause, leaving the stress outside. Then, in front of a mirror, look in your eyes, breathe and connect with dignity. Notice your posture and honor yourself by standing straight. Appreciate who you are. Give yourself a smile and a knowing wink.

Peace of mind comes with taking care of body, mind and soul. The clearer you understand yourself, the smarter your choices, and Life is happier. You are your best friend. Trust your gut.

Notice stress in your body, then release it in healthy ways:

- Connect with your safe place to protect and defend your Life.
- Pay attention to choices when eating, notice if they are satisfying and healthy.
- Relax more by stopping during the day to notice what you sense.

Simple physical exercises to relax stress:

- Get at least 30 minutes of moderate exercise. Be aware of

posture when you walk, sit or stand—hold your head high and your shoulders down and back. Look at where you are going. Smile more.

- When sitting—hold your chin up, bend your elbows and slowly flap your arms like a bird. Bend and straighten your legs. Rotate your feet several times in both directions and feel the stretch in your ankles. Do this at any time.

- Stretch out your arms and rotate your hands forward three times and backwards three times. Do it a few times and notice how good you feel.

- Do something fun.

- Do anything that puts a smile on your face; this includes, texting a friend, looking at photos of loved ones or even watching TV.

- Being happy, excited or content lowers levels of stress hormones that are linked to heart disease.

When the heart is at ease, the body is healthy.

Chinese Proverb

Sensual thinking is the immersive, interactive skill of thinking for yourself when everything changes. Stay true to yourself. No matter what is happening, things will come together. Stay open to the unexpected.

Words that we feel with our mind, like courage, dignity, freedom and curiosity, are the diet of wonder. Use them to know yourself better, fight injustice and find community. When thinking is clear, communication is harmony and bravery is common sense.

Life is a gift—the more it's savored the better it tastes. Savor the flavor!

Gratitude unlocks the fullness of life.
It turns what we have into enough, and more.
It turns denial into acceptance, chaos to order,
confusion to clarity.
It can turn a meal into a feast, a house into a home,
a stranger into a friend.
Gratitude makes sense of our past, brings peace for today,
and creates a vision for tomorrow.[21]

Melody Beattie

The 12-Step Program for Stress

A 12-step Program is a set of guidelines outlining a course of action for recovery from addictive or dysfunctional behavior. The pressures of stress create this unwelcome behavior without us realizing it.

1. Admit stress impacts your thinking, eating and overall health.

2. Realize, however good or bad a situation is, it will change. Use your senses and mind to analyze the environment and act to move forward and away from what is stressing you.

3. No one oversees your happiness but you. Make peace with your past so it can't screw up the present. You know what you're doing. Only you control your thinking.

4. To connect breathing with your mind and body, take a deep breath in and then exhale all the way. Pull the trigger and go to your safe place to renew your intuitive connection

with purpose and direction. Trust yourself.

5. Let your mind and body distract you from the emotional bully of stress. Read, exercise, or find someone to talk to. Develop a strategy based on ways to feel good about yourself when you're in a stressful environment. Use foresight.

6. Be patient with yourself. Focus on the next small steps with tenacity.

7. Depend on your tools to protect choices and maintain inner balance. By honoring yourself, you won't regret your choices in the morning.

8. Check-in with your secret place often to notice what you sense and use intuitive tools, especially dignity, tenacity and patience to filter choices. Reconnect with the image of your perfect healthy body.

9. Notice with your eyes, ears, mouth, nose and skin to sense natural boundaries. Smile more.

10. Tell a joke, listen to music, take a walk or exercise to distract and diffuse stress.

11. Talk less and sense more. Courage, determination, patience and dignity have boundaries but no limits. They are very real tools that relieve stress. Remember your trigger word and use it often.

12. Stress comes and stress goes. You are in control of your thinking. Choose to feel smart.

> Happiness is when what you think, what you say
> and what you do are in harmony.
>
> *Gandhi*

Factoids:

- Peppermint leaves have been used to ease headaches and aid digestion for more than 2,000 years. Peppermint oil is a key ingredient in many decongestants and in remedies for irritable bowel syndrome. Consider drinking peppermint tea instead of coffee after a big meal.

- Parsley is a natural diuretic and can ease premenstrual bloat. It also has high vitamin C content. Chewing parsley after eating a meal heavy with garlic, freshens your breath. The next time it's on your plate decorating your fish, chicken or potatoes, eat it.

There are many tips on the web for beating stress. Woman's Health lists nine foods "that will keep you calm."

- Almonds—about ¼ cup contains vitamins and anti-oxidants that boost our immune system.

- Pistachios—about a handful helps to lower stressed out blood pressure, according to a 2007 Penn State study.

- Walnuts—about ¼ cup is good for the heart anytime.

- Avocados—½ of one is very high in potassium, which reduces blood pressure, says the National Heart, Lung, and Blood Institute.

- Skim milk—up to four or more servings a day provides calcium that can reduce muscle spasms and soothe tension.

- Oatmeal— "Unsweetened, the slow steady digestion of carbs in the form of oatmeal creates a smooth steady flow of the relaxing brain chemical, serotonin," as stated by Judith Wurtman Ph.D., co-author of *The Serotonin Power Diet*. "Also, regular unprocessed oatmeal tends to keep us feeling full for hours."

- Oranges—high in vitamin C, plus a naturally sweet energy boost

- Salmon—a three-ounce serving is full of omega-3 fatty acids, which according to the Journal of the American Medical Association, protects against heart disease.

- Spinach—one cup provides magnesium which lowers stress levels as well as protecting our heart and our brain from stress related illness. It has one of the world's healthiest food ratings.

Popeye made himself super-strong by eating spinach. He may also have been protecting himself against osteoporosis, heart disease, colon cancer, arthritis, and other diseases at the same time.[22]

Give your stress wings and let it fly away.[23]

Terri Guillemets

Chapter 10

Satisfaction

Arriving at one goal is the starting point to another.[24]

John Dewey

Satisfaction is a feeling of achievement. It's a process, not a state of being. When you eat and pause to enjoy taste, there is a sense of satisfaction. This observation relaxes your body. At that moment, you are training your mind to notice healthy pleasure.

Satisfaction creates a sense of confidence and an aptitude in our mind for patience. It is the reinforcing positive experience that prepares our reasoning mind to respect challenges and the many steps it takes to surmount them.

Sensing makes us listen closer, look harder and want deeper. Sensual focus guides us to anticipate direction, priorities and boundaries that satisfy purpose. As satisfaction builds, we experience the power of patience. It is intuitive foreplay that leads to opportunity.

Actions we take and choices we make that feel satisfying re-establish our perception of natural momentum with the bigger picture. By noticing what you sense while you eat, you train your brain to tune-in to the experience of recognizing satisfaction and purpose along the path of Life.

By thinking sensually, you create a free zone of understanding, satisfaction and personal creativity to enjoy change. Life is adventure. Seeking satisfaction is part of our quest.

We are always working to track with what feels right. We want to stay clear to connect with dreams and purpose and turn them into reality. When you're searching and notice what you sense, pause. Be curious. Feel your intuitive tools. Courage, dignity, patience and tenacity are not the light at the end of the tunnel, they are the light inside teasing open your potential. Satisfaction waits around the corner.

> It always seems impossible until it's done.
>
> *Nelson Mandela*

Don't underestimate your intuitive muscles. They are the driving energy of personal character. The more you think with your senses, and depend on the tools, the more amazing the focus and understanding about yourself will be. To be inspired, notice what you sense. Life is full of surprises. It's a blend of splendor and responsibility. Dance with heart. You will find what you want.

> Stay close to anything that makes you glad you are alive.
>
> *Hafiz*

The intuitive quest for purpose is spearheaded by enthusiasm, dignity, humor, courage and self-respect. As we follow though, doing what feels right in the moment, it's easy to sense and benefit from the energy of satisfaction. There is rhythm to change.

Lucid living is the ability to create your dream and live it. It is being comfortably connected with winds of change and in sync with purpose. Your commitment to trust and to value what you sense directly connects to momentum that produces healthy satisfaction. It's a vitamin for self-discipline and hard work. Let yours work for you.

> When we create something, we always create it first in a thought form. If we are basically positive in attitude, expecting and envisioning pleasure, satisfaction, and happiness, we will attract and create people, situations, and events which conform to our positive expectations.[25]
>
> *Shakti Gawain*

Satisfaction we call success, begins as an idea and a plan. Stay curious and flexible. Being in the stream of change means trying unfamiliar choices and changing habits. Success can appear spontaneously from something unexpected.

Plan on succeeding. Your purpose is the inner connection with courage and confidence that gets stronger every time you notice it.

Nobody can understand how you feel because nobody is you. Yet amazingly, as you use intuition to focus on healthy choices, support comes to you from others.

If you get off to a fast start, but fail, then begin again. Depend on humor and patience. Trying something new is bold and often necessary. Satisfaction and accomplishment are worth the effort. The journey has many steps. We are always dancing. As you complete each step, be sure to recognize when it you feel satisfaction.

People are attracted to someone who has an attitude of moving ahead in life based on their own values. It's inspiring. Accept your lucid inner challenge. Your unique vibrant connection with character, style and personal power are coded for success.

Grace brings breathing room to understand and trust yourself. During the trial and error of learning to listen to that little voice, follow through. Physical and emotional satisfaction from lucid living naturally evolves. Stability is a blend of this satisfaction and momentum.

Everything changes. There are always surprises along the path of living that open our eyes, mind and heart. Actions generate satisfaction. Suddenly we re-connect with what matters. The fact is:

We are built to conquer environments, solve problems, achieve goals, and we find no real satisfaction or happiness in life without obstacles to conquer and goals to achieve.[26]

Maxwell Maltz

When answers are not satisfying, be curious. Use patience and self-discipline to pause for perspective. Balance what you think with what you know from experience. Confidence thrives on inner honesty.

When you need it, there is always an intuitive option. Your brain may be on overload, but your senses are alert. Use courage to be true to your truth. Life isn't fair, but you can be fair with yourself.

Sometimes feeling dissatisfied, we confuse hunger with what's really bothering us. Notice exactly what you sense and be curious about what drives you. You are in control of your choices. It's satisfying to protect yourself from destructive decisions.

Everyone has unique metabolic and hormonal make-up as well as unique stresses. Satisfaction is personal. Needs and tastes are different so a satisfying meal or comfortable choice will also be different.

Confusion is the unsatisfying yucky feeling of being off-balance. Intuitive tools nudge us to find balance and rhythm by remembering purpose and perspective.

For example, at mealtime:

(1) Tenacity and determination connect with a memory of the last time you ate something and it didn't satisfy. So, you become aware that you eat certain foods only out of habit.

(2) You take an intuitive pause, redirect your energy to decide if you're hungry or not, and realize you feel pressured to eat. It's not satisfying to eat because of pressure or when your body isn't hungry.

(3) You control your actions and decide not to eat.

Intuitive tools uncover habits that sabotage satisfaction. For example, procrastination caused by personal laziness can be the core of self-defeating flaws in reasoning. Putting off responding to signals from your body at mealtime is procrastination. Take the initiative and feed yourself wisely.

Inner dialogue is a glass-half-empty attitude of defeat that creates fear and doubts. Don't be trapped by it. When you notice inner dialogue creating pings in a good time or disrupting your connection with purpose, pull the trigger with an intuitive pause and sense your inner voice:

- Breathe to connect inner dignity and courage with your body.

- Use foresight to understand boundaries in the bigger picture.

- Use grace. The glass is half full. You are amazing.

- The next time you're in a funk, treat yourself like a celebrity.

Train your brain. Experiment. Learn what feels good. Have fun with variety; it's the spice of life. Use prudence, curiosity, patience, tenacity, foresight and determination to get what you need. Be brave. It's good to feel good.

Lucid living is self-reliant. Personal, emotional, spiritual, professional and nutritional needs are unique. Even in a great romantic relationship, we learn that no one person can give us everything we need to be happy. To stay satisfied, use curiosity, dignity and courage to dance to your own music and to try new choices.

> Personal satisfaction is the most important
> ingredient of success.[27]
>
> *Dennis Waitley*

Chapter 11

Tough Love

Open your eyes, look within.
Are you satisfied with the life you're living?[28]

Bob Marley

Tough love is a transparent compassionate commitment to do what is right—instead of what is easiest. Sensual thinking brings transparency to the nuances of love that keep the big picture in focus. There is no pause button on Life. Lucid living adapts to what's real with foresight and courage.

True love is honest. It is aware and strong, not always kisses. By sensing more, talking less, and following through, we bring out the highest qualities in those we love and ourselves. Perspective and dignity are points on our intuitive compass that point to love, while obstacles, opportunities and responsibilities keep us dancing to rhythms of change. Tough love has no problem with change. Every moment is new. Notice what catches your eye and what feels right.

There is absolutely no inevitability as long as there is
a willingness to contemplate what is happening.

Marshall McLuhan

We find love and understanding by listening for it. By tuning to your heart and being determined to notice what you sense, the bigger picture will come into focus. The greatest answers and joys in Life are very simple. Everything we need is sensual, especially love.

Even though love can be mysterious, it answers unspoken questions. Loving reminds us the impossible really does exist. Love is deep respect, and tough love takes Love seriously. Intuition is an inner drive of tough love, which boosts us to do, fix, change, have or allow. Confidence, empathy, tenacity and purpose are balancing beacons of love.

The beat of our hearts is a cosmic ritual that unites humanity. Your heartbeat is a steady rhythm of personal courage celebrating this moment with a Love that opens doors, but has no agenda. You were born to make history. Love has rhythm and balance. Listen to the music in your heart.

Think with your senses to thrive with the moments. Feel with your mind to know place and purpose in the bigger picture. Reason with courage and grace. It's simple to hear kindness, taste truth, touch moments and see love. Tough love always sees the bigger picture. Honor, morality, kindness and truth are transparent.

Everyone can learn from the past and stay clear about the present to open doors for the future. Take the initiative to give your family the experience of personal tough love. Introduce the determined self-control that is part wisdom, part survival. Mealtime is the perfect opportunity to teach children to use intuitive tools.

Parent with Sensual Thinking and Tough Love

Traditionally tough love refers to parenting choices and responsibilities. Teaching children to recognize what they notice with their senses will protect them throughout their lives. Intuitive tools are easy reasoning skills that are a foundation of an inner strength that protects us.

Sensual thinking keeps big-picture priorities clear in stressful situations. Since intuition is not emotional and feels like common sense, it's comfortable for children of all ages to relate to.

Every parent knows it's easier to give a child what s/he wants to eat, than to say "no" and follow through. It takes calorie burning energy and patience to do the right thing. Guiding those we love to do what is right, instead of what is easiest, saves them from angst and failure.

Talk about using intuitive tools to make healthy eating choices with adolescents and interest perks up because it makes sense. Sensual thinking opens communication that is interesting and not judgmental. Listen to your children before offering your opinion. Respect that's learned is respect that's earned. It goes both ways.

When kids realize that they are actually being heard, they're more careful and more open about what they say. When parents stretch to communicate with and understand children, they're able to let go of frustration and the resentment that may come with the responsibilities of parenting.

Adolescents are interested in learning to recognize signals that give them advantages and a sense of control, as they make Life decisions and deal with social pressures. Sharing mutual concerns may initially be a surprise. Our teenagers are original thinkers who are very aware that they're inheriting a damaged world. They are hungry for ways to deal with it.

No matter how old or young children are, they look to us as an example of how to handle Life's challenges. Speaking the truth is powerful Love. Choosing to be honest with yourself and live life lucidly with dignity and patience is inspiring stuff. Children struggle to be self-reliant in our self-indulgent world. The power of being honest is a potent foundation for satisfaction, Love, and success.

If your kids give you a hard time about the new eating lifestyle, laugh. Laughter is contagious. Keeping a sense of humor eases communication and makes kids less resistant to new ideas. With children especially, humor feels forgiving. Sometimes kids say or do things just for effect and when you laugh with compassion, it lets them laugh at themselves and this keeps the energy going. That gives you the opportunity to introduce your perspective about eating or nutrition without stress or guilt.

Communicating intuitive tools with children includes talking about your choices and struggles. It lets them know that you respect them, and that you respect yourself. This is priceless. Importantly, you open the door for your children to share their choices and struggles with you. Communicating values that bring balance and comfort, teaches children not to give up. It is liberating to understand that nothing is inevitable and the future is ours to create.

You want your kids to have every opportunity to succeed. You are using foresight to be clear that you don't want them to fall through the cracks because of ignorance or a lack of energy. Tough love teaches curiosity and prudence. Eating what makes nutritional sense gives all of us physical benefits of energy and health.

- Create a "Try Everything Once" rule to encourage your children to be curiously bold, but to do it with prudence, in moderation. A taste is just a teaspoon. Encourage them to be creative. You may find yourself tasting ketchup on a spoon or biting into a raw potato in the name of curiosity. Teaching intuitive tools encourages children's personal freedom with food and tells them they are in control of their thinking.

Children easily relate to the tools because they're instinctively searching to make sense of Life. Younger children, especially, are always very curious because it is intuitive to want to know the truth.

Teenagers are searching for answers to questions about the smartest ways to deal with Life and the world they're inheriting. Talking about intuitive tools and sharing eating goals with the kids, communicates that you have confidence in their abilities to think. It gives them a vocabulary that is universal and empowering. Sensual thinking helps them understand they can control their choices, personally and socially. This makes kids feel a little safer in our scary world.

Sharing determination to tell yourself the truth is using tough love with yourself. Letting your children know you do this teaches them, by example to have self-respect and self-reliance. It validates their search for personal truth. It's good to let your family know that they are responsible for their own satisfaction.

Honesty builds trust. People of all ages instinctively respond to it. Lucid living is a commitment to being honest, real and staying in the present. Teaching this to your family will protect your children and give you satisfaction for the rest of your Life.

Guide your family to think creatively and see the bigger picture by talking about values and goals.

Talk about the five senses. Point out protective messages we get from our senses 24/7. Ask if they ever have a gut feeling and what they think it means.

Teach them to follow their inner voice because it will never be self-destructive. For example, if they think intuition is telling them they need to eat an entire box of cookies or to smoke pot—they are lying to themselves. Be clear about the importance of being deeply honest with yourself. Mention the long-term impact of self-sabotage and disappointment caused by lying.

- Guide them to use intuitive tools to stay clear about their decision-making process around peer pressures and bullying.

- Let them know that you are aware media can be confusing or misleading. Talk about it. You'll be impressed by what children observe. They need the tools to filter what is real.

- Experience proves that ultimate satisfaction comes from within. We each hold the answers to our own questions. Talk with them about how they use curiosity and courage in their reasoning.

- Let your family know you hold the highest expectations for them.

Set a family standard based on sharing the intuitive tools:

- Curiosity opens doors for new ideas. It's an open mind with no judgement.

- Prudence shows there are options that are not obvious. It is like comparison shopping.

- Tenacity is being true to yourself. It is personal nobility and strength.

- Dignity builds pride and honor. It is a heart connection.

- Determination is a weapon against laziness and ignorance. It is tough love.

- Patience reminds us that it's helpful to step back and take a deep breath in and slowly let it out, especially when feeling confused or frustrated. We all need breathing room. There is always another way to see things.

- Foresight is intuitive self-defense, the natural way to protect yourself in every situation. Notice what you notice

- Self-discipline is being honest with yourself. It is self-respect, which is the dignified way to make healthy satisfying choices. It is intuition.

- Courage is always available when you need it. You can feel it in your heart.

- Grace is to appreciate your Life and to treat yourself and others with kindness and respect. Grace is forgiving. When you forgive your children, they learn to forgive you.

Factoids:

- Over the past 30 years, the plates, cups, glasses, and utensils have gotten much bigger. In the 1960's, a dinner plate was about 8 ½" in diameter. Today your plates are 12" in diameter. A 9" plate holds about 140 calories and a 12" plate holds about 350 calories.

- We are visual by nature. Big plates encourage overeating because they make the portions look smaller. Use 9" plates to serve your meals. Then, your family can put on the plate exactly the portion that is smart and satisfying. If you encourage them to look at their food, they will learn to recognize a healthy portion size.

Chapter 12

The Lucky Ones

Approximately 842 million people suffer from hunger and malnutrition worldwide.[29] Malnutrition is a leading cause of blindness and death for children. Extreme hunger is an epidemic in our time.

> The war against hunger is truly mankind's war of liberation.[30]
>
> *John F. Kennedy*

We are the Lucky Ones. While so many must obsess about eating to stay alive, we have food from nearly every culture at our fingertips. It is amazing, from pizza to fried rice, hot dogs to sausage, spaghetti to curried shrimp, an English muffin to a baguette, we have choices. Our variety is priceless. No matter what the season, there is always ice cream and no matter what the reason, we can eat turkey or we can eat cake. Yet today there is hunger around us on the streets in our own city, state, and country.

Our bodies are composed of individual organs, rivers of blood, mountains of muscle, bacteria, bones, millions of cells, flesh, a brain, etc. When one organ is sick, like the stomach, the rest of the body doesn't function well. If you stub a toe, it can totally throw you off balance. Altogether, your body is a whole world. Importantly, your instinct when your body is ill or hurt, is to heal it.

We are a global family who share hunger, curiosity and dignity. Cultural boundaries, generational issues and religious isolation are being broken down by technology. Around the web, we join like capillaries on the breast of time. Hunger for change personally, socially, environmentally and politically is part of healing our world. We are here to help each other. Clean food, air and water are bigger news than politics. The big picture is clear. We <u>need</u> each other.

Our gut tells us that all our lives are connected. Our instinct should be to heal what's hurt. When people are hungry, we cannot have peace in our world. A hungry person cannot reason, because he or she is driven to do anything to survive. Because of hunger, our world is not healthy.

A hungry man can't see right or wrong. He just sees food.[31]

Pearl S. Buck

In places where there is little or no choice about what to eat, people instinctively eat what their body needs. For example, poor people in the southern United States have been known to eat the local clay soil. Why? Because it is unusually mineral rich and will nourish them. When circumstances are desperate, people intuitively eat what their body needs.

We don't have to be desperate to eat what our body needs. But we should be honestly hungry and respond to our physical need for nourishment. There really is no choice for many people. We are lucky to have so many options.

With every blessing comes responsibility. Our blessing of food abundance means we are responsible to choose wisely what we eat. It also gives us a responsibility to help feed those who are hungry.

Make obsessing about food and eating, a positive and productive part of your life—think about the food needs of others.

Most of our citizenry believes that hunger only affects people who are lazy or people who are just looking for a handout, people who don't want to work, but, sadly, that is not true. Over one-third of our hungry people are innocent children who are members of households that simply cannot provide enough food or proper nutrition. And to think of the elderly suffering from malnutrition is just too hard for most of us. Unlike Third World nations, in our country the problem is not having too little—it is about not caring enough![32]

Erin Brockovich

Tuning in to feeding the hungry throughout the world is as simple as pushing a button on your computer, or as involved as you want to be. You have the tools. With dignity and courage, see beyond yourself. Feed your own natural social and emotional hunger by helping others get enough to eat. There is always balance. Awareness of everyday hunger in our world beyond our own three meals, guides us to recognize and celebrate the wonder of Life.

Personal transformation can and does have global effects.
As we go, so goes the world, for the world is us.
The revolution that will save the world is
ultimately a personal one.[33]

Marianne Williamson

Eating intuitively for health and energy is understanding that food is nourishment for sustaining Life. With empathy, we feel the hunger of others because we know our own hunger.

Feeding those who are hungry is giving the gift of Life. Working to end hunger creates your part of the ripple effect to heal our world. Here are ways to help:

feedingamerica.org

Feeding America used to be called Second Harvest. They have a food bank locator and up-to-date Hunger news. This excellent site offers all kinds of opportunities to get involved and interact with others.

bread.org

Bread for the world helps feed hungry people worldwide. It's easy to get involved. This is a wonderful international site where you can act to help feed others. It also keeps abreast of the politics of hunger so that you can help fight hunger by staying aware of assistance reforms or bills, and adding your voice.

mazon.org

Mazon means food in Hebrew. This Jewish-based organization collects food for local charities of all races, ages and religions and is committed to finding a long-term solution to end hunger internationally. Jeremy Piven and Michael Ian Black are donors and celebrity ambassadors. The site is very helpful, listing ways to be involved to nourish others.

feedthechildren.org

Feed the Children is an amazing and touching site that focuses on feeding children around the world, with an emphasis on rescuing abandoned children and a special focus on American children. They also provide food for families in need of nourishment. The site lists all kinds of opportunities to participate. Do it.

endhunger.com

The End Hunger Network works with the entertainment community to create and support media projects, programs and events to raise awareness and generate action to end childhood hunger. This program makes certain that people are eligible to receive food stamps from the government, and is connected to various projects working to eliminate the plight of hungry children. The site has a button to push that lists ways to get involved or volunteer at local hunger organizations. You just supply your zip code. John Travolta, Jeff Bridges and Tim McGraw are advocates for End Hunger.

> Thirty-five million people in the U.S. are hungry,
> or don't know where their next meal is coming from,
> and 13 million of them are children.
> If another country were doing this
> to our children, we'd be at war.[34]

Jeff Bridges

thehungersite.com

It doesn't cost anything, and a few minutes at The Hunger Site is a form of doing an intuitive pause. This site has been actively feeding people for FREE for over 10 years. Just a click provides a hungry person with food. It costs nothing to participate and does the world a lot of good. There is a tab on the hunger site that says Take Action! When you click on it, you will see a list of ways to help others. Please check this site out and participate.

About 24,000 people die every day from hunger or hunger-related causes. This is down from 35,000 ten years ago, and 41,000 twenty years ago. Three-fourths of the deaths are children under the age of five.

Famine and wars cause about 10% of hunger deaths, although these tend to be the ones you hear about most often.

The majority of hunger deaths are caused by chronic malnutrition. Families facing extreme poverty are simply unable to get enough food to eat. . . . It is estimated that one billion people in the world suffer from hunger and malnutrition.

mercycorps.org

Mercy Corps' partnership with The Hunger Site translates into lifesaving assistance for people in tremendous need around the world. When you visit, click, and shop at this unique site, you're making the future a little brighter for families who need food in the world's poorest places.

Dan O'Neill

Besides helping to feed others, the hunger site is a source of opportunities to:

> Provide mammograms—**nationalbreastcancer.org**

> Donate to causes related to children's health that are designed to connect people in simple ways to make the world a better place:
> **one.org** fights AIDS and extreme poverty
> **hki.org** fights and treats preventable blindness
> **pofsea.org** is a prosthetics outreach foundation

> Spread literacy—**roomtoread.org** works to break the cycle of poverty by teaching children to read;
> **firstbook.org** works to improve the quality of education for children nationwide.

> Save the rainforest—**worldlandtrust-us.org** buys land to preserve the rainforests.

nature.org The Nature Conservancy

> The Nature Conservancy's mission is to preserve the plants, animals and natural communities that represent the diversity of life on Earth by protecting the lands and waters they need to survive.

rainforestconservation.org

> The organization is working to expand the Reserva Comunal Tamshiyacu-Tahuayo in the Peruvian Amazon. This is supporting 14 species of primates, the most ever recorded in this region.

fundforanimals.org—Rescue animals.

The Fund for Animals operates four world famous animal care facilities, including the Cleveland Amory Black Beauty Ranch sanctuary in Murchison, Texas for abused and rescued animals, The Fund for Animals Wildlife Center in Southern California, the Cape Wildlife Center in Cape Cod, Massachusetts for the medical rehabilitation and treatment of injured wildlife, and the Rabbit Sanctuary for abandoned "pet" rabbits.

petfinder.com

Foundation provides relief in times of stress or disaster.

nsalamerica.org

North Shore Animal League America is a non-profit humane organization supported 100% by voluntary donations dedicated to finding the best possible home for each pet in its care, even if the pet is blind, deaf, or otherwise disabled. To date, the League has placed close to one million puppies, kittens, cats and dogs into carefully screened homes.

projecthealthychildren.org
hki.org
vitaminangels.org

Micro nutrients that we have, like iodine in our salt, folic acid in our flour or zinc, iron and vitamin A, can be added to water or food supplies in other parts of the world to prevent devastating, lasting and expensive birth defects.

Every minute, a child dies of malnutrition, and babies are

born deformed, blind or painfully damaged because their mothers were malnourished when they got pregnant. These organizations work to change that by providing essential nutrients for healthy children all over the world. The three URL's above are organizations you can work with to change the fate of innocent children. You can be a life saver.

A year's supply costs less than the cheapest hamburger. . . .
It's much cheaper to prevent birth defects
than to treat them[35]

Nicholas D. Kristof

DoSomething.org

A global movement of 5.5 million young people making positive change, online and off. Find out how to take action by visiting this site. Here are some facts:

- 11.3% of the world's population is hungry. That's roughly 805 million people who go undernourished daily, consuming less than the recommended 2,100 calories a day.

- The world produces enough food to feed all 7 billion people, but those who go hungry either do not have land to grow food, or money to purchase it. Fight hunger in your community by collecting food outside a local supermarket. Sign up for *Supermarket Stakeout GL*.

- 10 countries that have achieved greatest success in reducing the total number of hungry people in proportion to their national population are Armenia, Azerbaijan, Brazil, Cuba, Georgia, Ghana, Kuwait, Saint Vincent and Grenadines,

Thailand and Venezuela.

- Poverty is the principal cause of hunger. The causes of poverty include poor people's lack of resources, an extremely unequal income distribution in the world and within specific countries, conflict, and hunger itself.

- In 2010, an estimated 7.6 million children—more than 20,000 a day—died. Poor nutrition plays a role in at least half of these deaths.

- Nearly 98% of worldwide hunger exists in underdeveloped countries.

- Almost 1 in every 15 children in developing countries dies before the age of 5, most of them from hunger-related causes.

- While hunger exists worldwide, 526 million hungry people live in Asia.

- Over a quarter of the world's undernourished people live in Sub-Saharan Africa. Almost 1 in 4 people in this region is chronically hungry.

- When a mother is undernourished during pregnancy, the baby is often born undernourished, too. Every year, 17 million children are born this way due to a mother's lack of nutrition before and during pregnancy.

- Similarly, women in hunger are so deficient of basic nutrients (like iron) that 315,000 die during childbirth from hemorrhaging every year.

There are many ways to help others:

shoe4africa.org

Using racing as a vehicle, shoe4africa provides food, medicine access to education and more. The support provided by this organization enables the people of Kenya to keep their Dignity. They are empowering these people to rebuild their lives. This is beautiful. The site lists ways to participate.

Please watch these two clips. The first is about Kenya's first public children's hospital, which *shoes4africa* is building, and the second is about dignity in a refugee camp. On both clips, dignity and courage radiate from the children.

youtube.com/watch?v=DeiuZ1fbdRM

youtube.com/watch?v=0qnHV5_IHXU

firstgiving.com and justgiving.com (UK)

We exist to help you raise more money than you ever thought possible for the causes you care about. When we created the company in 1999, our dream was to enable any charity, however small, to use the web to raise money at very low cost.

mycharitywater.org

Right now, there are almost a billion people on the planet without clean and safe drinking water. Using *mycharitywater. org*, can help change that.

You can start a campaign to use your birthday; or create a competition to run, swim, walk or do just about anything to raise awareness and money for those in need. *mycharitywater.org* has a unique a fundraising model: 100% of all money raised goes straight to water projects. Every project is then proved with GPS coordinates and photos, and posted on Google Earth for you to see.

threesquare.org

The vision of Three Square is simple: No one in our community should be hungry. By bringing together the resources, experience and passion of the people and businesses of Southern Nevada, we can make sure no one has to. When we work together, we don't just serve food. We serve hope.

The food bank serves as a central collection and distribution center for donated, rescued and solicited food and grocery product. We provide bakery, produce, dairy, non-perishable products and ready-to-eat meals to non-profit and faith based organizations who serve those in need in our community. We also facilitate childhood and senior nutrition programs.

Celebrity Chef Kerry Simon holds threesquare.org very close to his heart. Despite his busy schedule, Chef Simon regularly fills backpacks on Friday afternoons so that local children, who would otherwise go hungry, can have food over the weekend. Go to the website to see how you can participate with or support Three Square.

mothersonamission.org and click on "DONATE"

Mothers on a Mission International is a group working together to mobilize others in helping underprivileged women and children in Kenya.

> We are restoring women and children to their dignity and destiny. We are raising up young leaders in communities around the globe. We are rescuing, restoring and rehabilitating street boys in Africa by building a school where they can live. We are providing business opportunities and resources for community development.

You will be amazed to discover there is always enough time to draw into your Life exactly what feels right.

Since Life doesn't come with a manual, we don't always know what we need. Being curious about the needs of others can shed light on your needs and path. Opportunities and options appear. If you work in soup kitchens for one meal a week, you're channeling your personal concerns about eating to feeding others and you'll learn about yourself and gain insight into your emotional relationship with food. When you help others, it enhances your Life in a way that creates wisdom. Wisdom becomes common sense and always connects with Love.

When we value curiosity and dignity, there is enough time to do the right thing. I live in NYC, and sometimes when I'm rushing, I see a blind person bravely navigating the stairs into the subway or an elderly person unsuccessfully trying to hail a taxi. It takes less than a minute to help these people and it allows me to stay connected with my 6th sense because it always—very quickly—feels right.

When we help those less fortunate, we recognize how lucky we are. When someone appreciates us, we pause to appreciate ourselves, without realizing it.

Perspective creates balance. Balance is that comforting feeling of being in control. By helping others, we are less self-centered and more balanced. And as we connect with others, we are enriched. Train your brain to be great by helping others.

I read about a woman who keeps a grocery bag handy, and every time she loses a pound, she puts a pound of canned food into the bag. When she collects 10 pounds, she donates it to the community food bank. This is a creative way to help others by using tenacity, dignity, patience and grace.

Our gut feeling is to be the best we can be, to live the best possible life. Sensual thinking boosts energy and creativity to help ourselves by helping others who are hungry. We are The Lucky Ones.

> The day hunger disappears, the world will see
> the greatest spiritual explosion
> humanity has ever seen.[36]
>
> *Federico Garcia Lorca*

Chapter 13

Sensual Syncing

We do not need Magic to transform the world.
We carry all we need inside ourselves already.

J. K. Rowling

In this Virtual Age, lucid living fills us with curiosity, determination and desire to live beyond who we have been. Between our reasoning mind and the deeper dimensions of sensual thinking is ripe multidimensional awareness and focus on resilience and purpose. It is the open door to engaging and interacting with the real world.

By sensing what is possible and thinking with our whole mind, we become *insanely* clear about direction. We are most productive and know inner peace when the focus of our eyes, ears, nose, mouth, flesh and mind, merge with the wisdom of our heart.

Sensual thinking is a natural evolution constantly sparked and refined by technology. It is inclusive, innovative and organic. Sensual syncing is a *shared vibration* that is the excitement and understanding of being in tune with change and each other. Boundaries and communication are clear. Like eye contact, it's instant to know what's real and what's not.

By sensing what you anticipate using intuitive tools—like

courage, curiosity, patience or tenacity—everything stays in focus. You gain powerful, practical awareness. It becomes automatic to update and fine-tune communication to collaborate efficiently, protect yourself and enjoy Life.

We are responsible for our thoughts and the consequences of our actions. If we make a mistake, there is always a price. But, we have intuitive tools for direction. They are the *free pass* that clears the way. They are the power of understanding how things come together. There are boundaries but no limits to what makes sense.

Sensual thinking connects the dots so that priorities are balanced by values and heart. Stay in-touch with the velvet depths of what feels right. Talk less, sense more. Consider evidence-based real-world solutions over blind ideology. Lucid living connects your imagination and sense of possibility with innovation, passion and wisdom to build new ways to solve problems.

> Major advances in civilization . . . all but wreck
> the societies in which they occur.
>
> *A. N. Whitehead*

Stay hungry for Life. Sync with change and take action in tune with what you value. You will be most productive and most relaxed by staying tuned to what's real.

The most important promise is the one you make to yourself when you feel most alive. Share your voice with others. Communicate, innovate and collaborate. What you choose to do can change everything.

> . . . Stay hungry, stay foolish.
>
> *Steve Jobs*

Bio

Jane Bernard is a visionary and a teacher trained to observe how people learn. She is passionate about the role of Sensual Thinking to facilitate enduring positive change in our world. Logical and original, Jane has been called *inspiring* and *provocative*. Through her eyes, we see ourselves differently.

Degrees in Philosophy (The New School) and Special Education (Bank Street College), combined with four decades of Rinzai Zen practice, and the "everyman college of living," all contribute to her philosophy.

Jane is a writer and the author of three books about intuitive thinking. She has been a guest on TV and international radio, at art galleries, schools and other venues talking from an intuitive perspective. Jane introduced her first book, *Fine Tuning*, on The Montel Williams Show, in 2006. Her second, *Knock Your Block Off!*, is written for writers. Jane's easy-going combination of common sense and originality is a natural eye-opener.

Her background includes working with autistic and learning-challenged children, educational think tanks, writing professor, a regular on national radio, technical writer, and coaching people to be intuitive eaters. People have been connecting with their senses to take control of eating habits since 2011, with her helpful book about intuitive eating, *Am I Really Hungry?*

Jane's dream is to produce multimedia happenings for each of the senses as edu-tainment events. She wants to give people a collaborative experience with sensual thinking. These will be opportunities to tap into our unique creativity for fun and to find new solutions for old problems.

She lives her philosophy. Jane discovered sensual thinking through hard lessons by ignoring her intuition. Since life is full of the unexpected, the unlikely, and the impossible, staying in-tune with change by thinking with her senses, is how she keeps an open mind.

Jane sees each person as a facet on the gem of humanity. For her, nature, music and travel are muses. She treasures kindness and character. Jane is thankful and inspired by the generous enthusiasm she receives from around the world.

She lives in Brooklyn, NY, goes to Bikram yoga, writes every day, consults schools about integrating intuitive thinking to enhance learning, and enjoys the energy of New York City. This sensual philosopher sees herself as a spark, so that others may flame.

Jane is a mother and a grandmother. She is a member of The Dramatists Guild of America, The Association for Conflict Resolution, The UN NGO IDP Education Peace Team (EPT), The International Speakers Bureau, The First Zen Institute of America, Independent Book Publishers Association, National Association of Professional Women, and The Groucho Club (UK).

NOTES

[1] Alan Cohen, www.brainyquote.com

[2] Jay Dixit, "How to Reprogram Mental Eating Habits for Physical Success," Psychology Today, July/August 2008

[3] General Dodonna, Star Wars, Dir. George Lucas, 1977

[4] Ingrid Kohistadt, Food and Nutrients in Disease Management. (Boca Raton, Florida: Taylor and Francis Group, 2009)

[5] J. K. Rowling, www.brainyquote.com

[6] Chandra Mohan Jain Osho, Institute for Integrative Nutrition, 2009, www.facebook.com/NutitionSchool/posts/10150944256996361

[7] Paul Fleming, www.GreatThoughtsTreasury.com

[8] Hippocrates, www.goodreads.com

[9] https://www.dukedietandfitness.org/outpatient-services/diet-and-nutrition

[10] Henry Ford, www.brainyquote.com

[11] Dr. Michael Lutter, 2008, www.utsouthwestern.edu/newsroom/news-releases/year-2008/hunger-hormone-increases-during-stress-may-have-antidepressant-effect-researches-report.html

[12] Andrew Weil, M.D., www.thinkexist.com

[13] Harriet Brown, "Go with your gut," The New York Times, 2006: www.nytimes.com/2006/02/20/opinion/20brown.html

[14] Arden, Paul, It's Not How Good You Are, It's How Good You Want to Be. (London: Phaidon Press Ltd., 2003)

[15] Janet Rae-Dupree, "Can You Become a Creature of New Habits?" New York Times, May 4, 2008

[16] Ibid.

[17] St. Francis de Sales, www.brainyquote.com

[18] St. Francis de Sales, www.brainyquote.com

[19] Jonathan Larson, http://majannmariedaneker.blogspot.com/2009/01/how-do-you-measure-year.html

[20] Dr. Michael Lutter, 2008, op. cit.

[21] Melody Beattie, www.thinkexist.com

[22] http://www.whfoods.com/genpage.php?tname=foodspice&dbid=43

[23] Terri Guillemets, www.finestquotes.com/author_quotes-author-Terri%20Guillemets-page-0.html

[24] John Cook, The Book of Positive Quotations, (Minneapolis: Fairview Press, 1996)

[25] Shakti Gawain, en.thinkexist.com

[26] Maxwell Maltz, 1899-1975, thinkexist.com

[27] Dennis Waitley, www.brainyquote.com

[28] Bob Marley, 1945-1981, www.finestquotes.com

[29] https://borgenproject.org/15-world-hunger-statistics/

[30] John F. Kennedy, 1917-1963, www.betterworld.net/quotes/endhunger-quotes-3.htm

[31] Pearl S. Buck, 1892-1973, http://www.betterworld.net/quotes/endhunger-quotes.htm

[32] Erin Brockovich, http://www.betterworld.net/quotes/endhunger-quotes.htm

[33] Marianne Williamson, http://www.brainyquote.com/

[34] Jeff Bridges, http://www.betterworld.net/quotes/endhunger-quotes.htm

[35] Nicholas D. Kristof, "The World's Healthiest Food," New York Times, January 3, 2010

[36] Federico Garcia Lorca, 1898-1936, http://www.azquotes.com/quote/570362

Made in the USA
Columbia, SC
25 July 2017